Gerlac Petersen

The fiery soliloquy with God, of the Reverend Master Gerlac Petersen

In which are pointed out the solid and clear paths of the whole spiritual life

Gerlac Petersen

The fiery soliloquy with God, of the Reverend Master Gerlac Petersen
In which are pointed out the solid and clear paths of the whole spiritual life

ISBN/EAN: 9783741190681

Manufactured in Europe, USA, Canada, Australia, Japa

Cover: Foto ©Lupo / pixelio.de

Manufactured and distributed by brebook publishing software (www.brebook.com)

Gerlac Petersen

The fiery soliloquy with God, of the Reverend Master Gerlac Petersen

THE
FIERY SOLILOQUY WITH GOD.

(Copyright reserved.)

𝕸𝖊𝖉𝖎𝖆𝖛𝖆𝖑 𝕷𝖎𝖇𝖗𝖆𝖗𝖞 𝖔𝖋 𝕸𝖞𝖘𝖙𝖎𝖈𝖆𝖑 𝖆𝖓𝖉 𝕬𝖘𝖈𝖊𝖙𝖎𝖈𝖆𝖑 𝖂𝖔𝖗𝖐𝖘.

THE
𝕱𝖎𝖊𝖗𝖞 𝕾𝖔𝖑𝖎𝖑𝖔𝖖𝖚𝖞 𝖜𝖎𝖙𝖍 𝕲𝖔𝖉,

OF THE REVEREND
MASTER GERLAC PETERSEN,
OF DEVENTER, CANON REGULAR,
AND CONTEMPORARY WITH THOMAS A KEMPIS,

IN WHICH ARE POINTED OUT

𝕿𝖍𝖊 𝕾𝖔𝖑𝖎𝖉 𝖆𝖓𝖉 𝕮𝖑𝖊𝖆𝖗 𝕻𝖆𝖙𝖍𝖘 𝖔𝖋 𝖙𝖍𝖊 𝖜𝖍𝖔𝖑𝖊 𝕾𝖕𝖎𝖗𝖎𝖙𝖚𝖆𝖑 𝕷𝖎𝖋𝖊.

TRANSLATED FROM THE ORIGINAL LATIN,

BY A SECULAR PRIEST,
AUTHOR OF A TRANSLATION OF
"The Book of the Visions and Instructions of B. Angela of Foligno;"
"The Life of V. Grignon de Montfort;" etc., etc.

𝕺𝖚𝖗 𝕷𝖆𝖉𝖞 𝖔𝖋 𝖙𝖍𝖊 𝕾𝖆𝖈𝖗𝖊𝖉 𝕳𝖊𝖆𝖗𝖙, 𝖕𝖗𝖆𝖞 𝖋𝖔𝖗 𝖚𝖘.

𝕷𝖔𝖓𝖉𝖔𝖓:
THOMAS RICHARDSON AND SON;
DUBLIN AND DERBY.
NEW YORK: HENRY H. RICHARDSON AND CO.
1872.

["Nullum etiam evidentius judicium et signum est unionis cum Verbo, quam sic absque ulla augustia in interiori latitudine conversari in communi amore, omnia dantes, omnia replentes cum Jesu. Sic quantum in nobis est, possumus implere cœlum et terram et omnia quod in eis sunt, amore nostro qui Deus est."—chap. xxxvi.

TO

The Holy Ghost,

THE COMFORTER,

[WHO

BRINGETH BACK TO OUR MIND ALL THINGS,

WHATSOEVER THE

WORD OF LIFE HATH SAID.

APPROBATIONES

Ignitum hoc cum Deo Soliloquium, conscriptum a R. Gerlaco Petri, Can. Regulari Windesemensi ante ducentos annos, succinctam et certam ostendens viam perveniendo ad summam perfectionem, quæ consistat in unione cum Deo per amorem: mirabiliter expedit, ut in lucem prodeat, et a quocumque Christiano homine legatur. Sic attestor ego Gisbertus Coevrinck, Decanus Ecclesiæ S. Joannis Evangelistæ Busco ducensis, S. Theol. Licentiatus, librorum Censor. 3 April. Anno Domini, 1613.

Ignitum hoc cum Deo Soliloquium pulcherimis rationibus seu igniculis quibusdam animos a confusa rerum multitudine abstractos ad intimam cum simplicissima monade inflammat, nec Catholicæ contradicat fidei, aut morum honestati repugnat.

Scriptum Colon. 22 Febr. 1616.

HENR. FRANCKEN-SIERSTORPFFIUS,

SS. Theol. D. Gymn. Laurent.

Regans, Librorum Censor.

TRANSLATOR'S PREFACE.

THE "Fiery Soliloquy with God" is the work of the Reverend Master Gerlac Petersen, of Deventer, Canon Regular, and contemporary with Thomas à Kempis. Indeed, so full of the spirit of the supposed author of the "Following of Christ" is this little work, that although, unlike the latter, addressed more perhaps to the intellect than to the heart, its writer was known in old times as "Alter Thomas de Kempis." The Cologne edition of the Soliloquy, 1616, was published under this title.

Gerlac Petersen, Canon Regular of the Order of S. Augustine, was born at Deventer in the year 1378. He spent his youth in the college of that city, which had been established by the celebrated Master Florentius Radewyns, Canon of Utrecht, and disciple of Gerard Groot.

Born only two years before Thomas à Kempis, they must have passed their boyhood together, and studied not only Grammar and plain chant, but that truer science of holiness, which alone, in the highest sense of the word, ennobles man by separating him from all that is not God, and uniting him with his Creator. After having finished his studies he entered the monastery of Windesheim, near Zwoll, where he received the religious habit in 1403. From the day of his spiritual espousals to the hour of his death, his life seems to have been one onward march towards a fuller vision of the face of Christ, so far as it could be enjoyed in this world. Let us hear what a former editor of the Soliloquy says about him.

"He was a man venerable in all things, in face like unto an angel, in manner pleasing, in speech sweet, ever lifted up above the things of earth by his fruition of God. The holy joy of his soul, and his interior devotion, shone even outwardly upon his body. Illuminated by God with the spirit of wisdom and understanding, he was inflamed with an earnest desire to know himself, to search into the truth, and to contemplate heavenly things.

"Towards the end of his life he suffered beyond measure from a very painful disease, but nothing could overcome his patience, or his spirit of thanksgiving; his constant prayer being, that in this life he might have his purgatory. He rested in our Lord, with Whom he had been ever inwardly united, on the octave of S. Martin's Feast, in the year 1411."

Besides the "Fiery Soliloquy," Gerlac Petersen is said to have written two other little works, "*Breviloquium de accidentiis externibus*," and "*De Libertate Spiritus.*" The "Fiery Soliloquy" may be said to represent the intellectual side of the asceticism of the school of Deventer, just as the "Following of Christ," on the supposition that it was written by Thomas à Kempis, may be said to represent the sanctification of the affections, as taught in that celebrated school of spirituality. The distinguishing features of both these sides may be summed up in the two great spiritual gifts: intellectual humility and unselfish love of God, the result of which is liberty of spirit. In Gerlac's writing we can clearly trace the influence of Gerard Groot, as well as of Ruysbroek, whose advice had greatly assisted Gerard in all his plans. In translating the "Fiery Soliloquy" into English, as a contributor to the "Mediæval Library of Mystical and Ascetical Works," the translator has been moved by a desire to make English-speaking Catholics acquainted with a sterling work of the Middle Ages, which seems to have been almost forgotten. He believes that this little work will be found to fulfil the promise of its title, and in a short space to point out the solid and clear paths of the spiritual life. There are indeed in places certain expressions which require explanation, but it is earnestly hoped that in the note to chapter xvi. sufficient information has been given to clear up any difficulty or doubt that may arise in the reader's mind. To the translator the "Fiery Soliloquy" seems one of the most unselfish spiritual works he has ever read.

The original Latin is somewhat difficult and cramped, and at times the translator has felt in considerable doubt whether he has accurately seized the meaning of the holy writer. Still, with all its imperfections, he believes that his translation may be taken on the whole as a trustworthy rendering of the original work. The text which he has adopted is that of Cologne, 1616, with the exception that, following Strange's example in his edition published in the same city in 1849, he has placed the thirty-sixth chapter after the fourth.

May that Blessed Spirit, Who turns the hearts of the children to the fathers, accompany this translation of a work written in ages long gone by, that all who read it may find, in the midst of our selfish and over-busy modern life, refreshment for their souls, together with that peace of God which passeth all understanding.

Our Lady of the Sacred Heart, pray for us.

CONTENTS.

	PAGE
The First Chapter.—That he who would recover his heart from dissipation should look ever to the end of all things, and refuse to be consoled by anything out of God ...	2
The Second Chapter.—That man should frequently look to his state of exile, and take refuge in God, united to Whom he will want for nothing	5
The Third Chapter.—That in whatever we have to do, we should ever look to the end for which it should be done, especially in the Divine Office	8
The Fourth Chapter.—With how great devotion we ought to be present at the Divine Office, and above all at the Sacrifice of the Mass	9
The Fifth Chapter.—Of the fruit of all ceremonies and outward Sacraments	11
The Sixth Chapter.—That virtue is to be practised only for the love of virtue, because it is always good	13
The Seventh Chapter.—That with true humility, and with our eyes fixed upon the truth, ought we to resist vain thoughts and vicious motions	14
The Eighth Chapter.—That by selfishness or self-seeking the interior course of the soul is hindered	17
The Ninth Chapter.—Of true liberty, or of the beatitude of the deiform soul	20

	PAGE
The Tenth Chapter.—Of the fruit of holy liberty, and the glory of the deiform soul	23
The Eleventh Chapter.—How the interior look of a man becometh clear and enlightened, and his exterior innocent and simple, and how the whole man is made deiform	26
The Twelfth Chapter.—Of the hidden sweetness of the spiritual cross, and what it is to persevere therein, and what a man ought to know concerning it	32
The Thirteenth Chapter.—How interior vices, together with the devil their chief, never cease to lay snares for the soul that loveth God	44
The Fourteenth Chapter.—That the interior man, both in the presence and in the absence of grace, maketh profit and increase, and how he is taught by the Angels in what way he should stand in the Presence of God	51
The Fifteenth Chapter.—That by the love of God true security is infused into a man	62
The Sixteenth Chapter.—That to love justice and truth, and in all things to seek the glory of God, is to abide in the cross of our Lord	66
The Seventeenth Chapter.—That the soul, free from everything belonging to itself, is everywhere secure in God ...	69
The Eighteenth Chapter.—Of the exercise of the spiritual man, especially of the Religious in the Divine Office ...	73
The Nineteenth Chapter.—That nothing is sweeter or more glorious than for the soul to inhere in the Highest Good, and to become conformed to the Holy Trinity	76
The Twentieth Chapter.—How to a devout man his highest good is to be with God, and his greatest evil to be without God	81
The Twenty-first Chapter.—The prayer of a man, whose soul is clouded, for the illumination of his heart	83

The Twenty-second Chapter.—That he who is truly poor in

	PAGE
spirit should glory in his poverty, and in his own nothingness ...	85
The Twenty-third Chapter.—Of true self-resignation	88
The Twenty-fourth Chapter.—How he who is poor in spirit is exceeding rich ...	92
The Twenty-fifth Chapter.—How blessed a thing it is to rise in soul above every outward exaltation, and to sink below every humiliation ...	96
The Twenty-sixth Chapter.—Of the double region, that is, of the lower region of sensuality, and the higher, of the reformed soul ...	99
The Twenty-seventh Chapter.—How strictly God will require the reformation, or the amelioration, as well of our interior as of our exterior ...	111
The Twenty-eighth Chapter.—Exhortation to conform ourselves to the image of God ...	114
The Twenty-ninth Chapter.—The heritage of the poor in spirit in this life ...	116
The Thirtieth Chapter.—Of the praise of holy poverty, and how by voluntary bearing of adversity we arrive at the clarification of the soul ...	117
The Thirty-first Chapter.—In what way the interior man is clarified, and united with the Word, and that in whatever happeneth, and in all we do, we have need of a simple eye and a pure intention ...	132
The Thirty-second Chapter.—That virtue in itself standeth unchangeable, nor doth it lie under the power of any accidents ...	134
The Thirty-third Chapter.—That besides God nothing can truly comfort the soul ...	140
The Thirty-fourth Chapter.—That by the strength of the soul the weakness of nature must be sustained ...	143
The Thirty-fifth Chapter.—That contemplation is never joined with commotion and disturbance ...	147

	PAGE

The Thirty-sixth Chapter.—That our Lord Jesus is to be looked at in a two-fold way, and of the efflux of love ... 149

The Thirty-seventh Chapter.—That reproof is to be borne with evenness of mind, whether it be just or unjust ... 153

The Thirty-eighth Chapter.—That all men in general are to be embraced in truth and love 156

The Thirty-ninth Chapter.—What it is that chiefly unburdeneth and rendereth the heart free 159

HERE BEGINNETH THE

Fiery Soliloquy with God,

OF THE

REVEREND MASTER GERLAC PETERSEN,

WHILE ENDEAVOURING TO WITHDRAW HIS
HEART FROM MANY OBJECTS TO
THE ONE HIGHEST GOOD,

AND FIRST OF ALL THROUGH PRAYER.

IN the spirit of lowliness, and with a broken and humbled heart, and as the dust of the feet under heaven and earth and all things therein, we fall down before Thee, and hoping nothing in any way from ourselves, but full of humble hope in Thee, even as some poor little lamb or lonely wandering chicken we take refuge beneath Thy wings, and ask that we may be ever received by Thee in mercy, O most gracious Father!

Chapter I.

That he who would recover his heart from dissipation should look ever to the end of all things, and refuse to be consoled by anything out of God.

IN all things that happen unto me, and that either do move me or might move me, I will always look to the end; that is to say, I will cast over in my mind, if now at this instant I were to be called by our Lord how I should feel or stand in that matter which moveth me. And wheresoever I am an obstacle in my own way, a hindrance or a veil between myself and God, there it behoveth me to say to myself or to any other such object: "Get thee behind me, Satan; thou art a scandal unto me before the Lord."* Thus there-

---

* Matt. xvi. 23.

fore will I exercise myself within, and show myself without, as if all my behaviour, movements, and conversation were crying out and bearing witness that " my kingdom is not of this world,"* and that here I have no comfort or solace whatsoever. And thus will I remain in all things which happen unto me, even unto the end of my life, "as a vessel that is destroyed," as dead to the world, as " the refuse of the world,"† as unconsoled and forsaken by everything that is in the world, as unworthy of the least gift of God whether corporal or spiritual, or even to kiss the dust of the feet of God's elect. And even as I shall be unconsoled and forsaken by all things in the world, so nevertheless let all things be forsaken by me, so that being poor, I may be able in great inward breadth, without any hurt, to suffer want of all things which the mind of man can desire, out of or except God Himself. Nay, even if all things should happen according to my desire or con-

---

* Joan. xviii. 36.   † I. Cor. iv, 13.

venience, yet let "my soul refuse to be comforted;"* for it is my choice thus to lie hidden all the days of my pilgrimage, living like a true pilgrim and naked traveller, that I may be able to look in all security for the day of the Lord; most rich the while, and at the same time most poor, most rich in seeking nothing, most poor in having nothing. So too in no way will I set myself above anything or any living being, but I will strive in all things to be inwardly well united with our Lord, because all things pass away, and come to nothing. For if I should have leant upon that which falleth to decay, then I too must needs fall away together with it, both I and it, for "vain are the sons of men,"† and hardly in any one of them is to be found faith that never faileth.

---

* Ps. lxxvi. 3.   † Ps. lxi. 10.

Chapter II.

That man should frequently look to his state of exile, and take refuge in God, united to Whom he will want for nothing.

NEVER will I forget, that continually am I placed in a state of pilgrimage, exile, struggle, conflict and war, even so long as the breath shall remain in my body. So shall I have no difficulty as to where, whence, and how, I may be supported during the short time of my sojourn upon earth. And if only I am able to attain to this, namely, to stand in the sight of our Lord, having all things in common with Him, within a pure heart; freed from all care as to the things of others, and subject to no disturbance of mind, what is there more that I can desire? But on the other hand, even if all things were mine, and my name were praised by many, and yet it did not go well with me with our Lord, what would it profit me? Let this man therefore be solicitous and trust in that man, another in another, yet will I offer myself unto our Lord, and trust in Him with my whole heart, nor will I be anxious about anything else whatsoever, or about any accidents which may happen, save only that I may be all His; for He it is Who provideth for me, and "He hath care of me;"* and He also it is Who hath given me commandment to empty myself of all that I am for His sake, and not to take upon myself His own work, nor to hinder that work in me by anxious care about what may happen, but to listen to what He Himself, Who is the Highest Good, is saying within me. "Labour," He saith, "as much as in thee lieth, to stand well with Me, and to walk before me at all times and in every place and cause; whether in these thou pleasest thyself or

---

* I. Pet. v. 7.

others, have no care, for the good pleasure of others can do thee no good, neither can their displeasure take aught away from thee, because if thou shalt abide in me, thou wilt be able to do without everything without hurt to thyself, and yet thou wilt want for nothing. Dost thou not consider that likeness and equality are only found in things that are like and equal? Or dost thou not know that true glory standeth in no need of vain glory? For virtue abideth ever in the highest, nor doth it stand in need of praise or favourable witness from those who are inferior, but is ever sufficient for itself. So also are all they who by a most burning love are made one with virtue itself."

Chapter III.

That in whatever we have to do, we should ever look to the end for which it should be done, especially in the Divine Office.

UNLESS with much inward labour a man study continually to look into everything which is to be done, that is to say, into the end for which it exists, and ought to be done, especially in the Divine Office, very easily, before he knows it, will he slide downwards into a state of dulness to interior lights; and it will appear to him enough to have leaves without the fruit. And weighed down in this way the soul will be unable to lift itself up, or direct itself towards Him Who alone is its origin, and in consequence of the greatest possible opposition arising from dissimilarity and thick darkness, to gaze upon the light which is incomprehensible, for the enjoyment of which however it was alone created. In all things therefore that we have to do let us accustom ourselves always to look at the truth, and to see how the truth looks at all things, and to conform ourselves to this look according to our measure, and to follow very diligently by a keen-sighted gaze the interior pathway to the Highest Good.

Chapter IV.

With how great devotion we ought to be present at the Divine Office, and above all at the Sacrifice of the Mass.

WITH a love and an affection like unto that with which our Lord Jesus Christ chose to become Man for our sakes, and to converse here amongst us in this wretched state of pilgrimage as the least and the poorest of all, in want, in tears, in sighs, and labours all the days of His Life, in persecutions, in most exceeding humble tolerance of evils and of proud adversaries, by spending His whole self for us both in body and soul; in a word, with a love like unto that incomprehensible love which He bore towards us, and with which He offered Himself for us upon the cross to the Eternal Father, a living victim, holy and without spot, in order that He might bring back with joy upon His shoulders the sheep which He had lost; even with such a love, and not with less doth He offer Himself for us day by day without ceasing, and above all upon the Altar. And although the aforesaid proofs of love were shown forth once for all from without, yet every moment are they as newly given in the Father by the Son together with the Holy Ghost, as when they were shown forth from without; and so also ought all the proofs of love which our Lord Jesus condescended to show forth in His own time for our salvation to be daily received by us, as if now at this very instant they were being done for the first time.

Chapter V.

Of the fruit of all ceremonies and outward Sacraments.

KEENLY to discern all things, and to transfuse ourselves, so far as is possible, into a certain pure, essential fruition of simple truth, to enter into and in a certain way to be transformed into oneness with love, and thus wholly constituted out of ourselves; to be moved to desire the good and the advantage of everyone, no less than our own; with very great devotion and the utmost reverence outwardly to receive the Holy Sacraments, and inwardly to taste in an efficacious manner their fruit and power, so that we may be one with Christ, and abide in Him, and He in us; it is for the sake of this union and mansion that all has been done that is done, and herein lies the fruit, effect, and end of all things, namely, that the soul may be led back to its own first original principle, which is God Himself. To perform every kind of good, to suffer every kind of evil that may happen, this is the real life of a Christian man. All other things whatsoever are reached from without, whether they be to exalt or to humble us, and all pass away with time, for which cause no great care is to be taken about them. But let us study vigorously and fervently to operate on the grace which hath been given us, and concerning all other dispositions of the Lord towards ourselves or others to remain undisturbed. Moreover, whatsoever the Lord hath been unwilling to give or hath not given, this let us leave to Him, and not give it to ourselves.

Chapter VI.

That virtue is to be practised only for the love of virtue, because it is always good.

IN no way will I show forth humility, abstraction, custody of the senses, modesty and simplicity merely as it were, on the surface, that is to say, merely because perhaps I am known, or out of fear of others, which is a motive full of anguish; for if I shall do this, as time goeth on perchance the reason for which I behaved in this or that way shall fail in me, and then I shall become unstable, and very inconstant, and I shall sink into levity or sorrow according to outward accidents. But in sincerity by looking at the truth will I perform these good actions and others like to them, knowing that not only now, but even unto the end of my life, such actions are acceptable before

God. And therefore in these and like virtues will I strive to make continual progress. Yea, it will be the part of a gentle and kind man to soften, when reason demands it, the importunities and disturbances of others rather by modesty and calm behaviour than by words. Yet very gently and patiently ought we to bear with one another in all things which are done less perfectly and orderly from without or from within; for to every one is his own calamity which he suffereth sufficiently grievous, whether it be of body or of mind.

Chapter VII.

That with true humility and with our eyes fixed upon the truth ought we to resist vain thoughts and vicious motions.

WHEN I look into myself in the light of truth and justice I am conscious that there is no good in me; for I see that I am of myself nothing but what is abominable, and that I am turned away from God and from the truth, and am in all things vanity itself; for I have stained the image of God within my soul, and even if it hath been formed again or renewed as to its proper form, yet have I had nothing to do with all this, but the whole work is the Lord's, that through all things and in all things it may be the loftiness of the power of God, and not from me. Whatever now springeth up in me of thought or movement that agreeth not with the sense of truth is accursed vanity and an abomination before God. Wherefore nowise will I pass over or hide such secret motions, as if I of my own self were anything at all, but I will strive to lower myself ever more and more and humble myself, and by looking not how my being exists in God, but by looking into the truth of my nothingness in myself, I will vigorously overturn them, that they may know that they are not truth and justice, but vanities and lies, nay even the devil himself. For whenever a man that is faithful unto the Lord shall have felt the movements of his own pride, or of the desire of pleasing others, or of an interior but unpurified feeling of exultation at the gifts of God, or of fear of giving displeasure, or of any other desire; straightway the purity of his sight is blunted and obscured at least on one side. And if he shall have cast a keen glance, he will see clearly that by these motions a veil as it were is stretched between him and the truth; that doubt, perplexity, and scrupulosity are increasing; for these motions, in whatever manner they may have arisen, bring such things along with them; nay, they themselves are nothing else but these. And he will feel that his trust in God is lessened, and this as long as he must needs suffer, until his vanity pass away before the face of truth. Humility therefore and truth are alone safe, and whatsoever is outside them is narrow and full of fear. Indeed, all other things are low and sunk down far away from the face of truth, nor have they ever stood upright; but not as yet doth truth so rule in the soul, as to enable it to see and feel that they have been brought down almost to nothing.

Chapter VIII.

That by selfishness or self-seeking the interior course of the soul is hindered.

THAT I am unable to follow what is high and broad and deep and incomprehensible, and to reach the wide, spacious, supreme heights of affective love, which exceed in innumerable ways the whole of creation, I have a clear proof in the fact that I am still held back and hemmed in by my own self-seeking, or that I find my rest in what is convenient, and dread what is inconvenient, and also to be humbled or not cared for. But with diligence will I find out, when I am crippled in my interior ascent, whether it be meet that I should be hemmed in by such a cause or not. If not, then speedily and freely will I pass beyond it; for not easily ought the state of our mind or the interior ascent of our spirit to be shaken or held back. For it is our Lord Jesus Himself Who enlighteneth us from within, and what is there which can blind us? It is our Lord Jesus Who giveth inward peace, and what is there which can give us trouble? It is our Lord Jesus Who maketh our interior ascent to be rapid and free, and what creature, or what opposition or adversity can depress or cripple it? "'*I am the Lord*,' He saith, '*Who sanctify My sanctuary:*'* nor do I suffer it to be transformed, but I give a holy rest in the midst of tumults, and I permit not that any strange forms or images should enter into or even rest in My Holy Temple. For I deem not anything to be worthy to hinder or depress a soul that is united unto Me. And very blameable do I judge it, that the soul itself should be busied with what is vile and useless, or with vain cares about future events, which

---

* Levit. xxi. 15.

perchance may never happen, when all the while it may freely enjoy its own nobleness in its own fontal origin." Let the soul therefore study, as far as it is able, not to be delayed by those things which are from below; and as to those which are above there is nothing to fear, for since not only is it not depressed by these, but is even more frequently and in different ways invited to stand with them in the presence of our Lord, and to walk in that interior and higher breadth and largeness of spirit, in which no narrowness is found, but the free and deiform gaze, which suffereth not the eye of the heart to be clouded over or to become blear.

Chapter IX.

Of true liberty or of the beatitude of the deiform soul.

"KNOW ye not," saith the deiform spouse herself, speaking in the spirit of truth, "how by grace I have received the power of presenting myself without form, appearing, as it were, naked and bare before the Face and the Presence of the eternal incommutable Truth, and intransmutable Identity, which is ever that which it is?" This indeed it is which alone truly goeth out to all things by outward procession, but which inwardly remaineth whole. Moreover, it is in the power of the deiform spouse to strip herself naked of all forms and images, and look into the Very Truth and Superessence of all beings throughout all creation. For there is not anything which she looketh at

as simply nothing, but in all things doth
she see God, as in the greatest so in the
least. Nothing therefore can easily transform such a soul so as to do it hurt.
But if good and pure images cannot
lightly do this, how much less shall everything which can darken or disturb the
soul prevail? Lastly, the soul thus rendered free by its fetters being broken,
and strengthened in virtue, is not less
blessed and endowed with virtue, abroad
than at home, in the midst of the crowd
than in solitude, in labour than in rest, in
prosperity than in adversity, and so also
in other like things that happen to it:
inasmuch as it is no less present with the
Very Truth here than there, and this
chiefly because being united with a most
burning love to Truth and Blessedness
(so far as this is possible) it is made partaker of the same. Now the true and
holy liberty of the soul consists in this:
First, to love nothing in this world, nor to
be honoured nor held in good repute, nor
one's own convenience in time or in eternity. So too that it should not rest even

in necessary exercises, nor be agitated impurely in its appetite by the desire of any creature whatsoever; for it is able, without pain, to be in want of all the things which it seemeth to have, because truth standeth in need of nothing, nor is it conscious of any loss of its own light. Secondly, that it should dread no difficulties or inconveniences, that is to say, neither labours nor sorrows, and that even in the absence of these things their memory should not oppress or torture the mind; that also in all reproofs, reproaches, and threats, it should be moved or disturbed by no grief or useless shame, but that it should draw down these things upon itself so far as truth itself shall dictate or show, but no more.

Chapter X.

Of the fruit of holy liberty, and the glory of the deiform soul.

BEHOLD, saith the Lord, I have given thee a face to look over against My face, and whatever in thee is deiform, and taketh up into its own self (in so far as it can) My Beauty and conformity with Me, that too have I given thee. And I have given thee the well-ordered conversation of thy outward man, which is more powerful than the countenances of all those who make war against thee, most of all those who resist thy spirit: so that they shall not be able to stand, nay, nor even to appear before thy mature and naked look, by which thou oversteppest all obstacles, and art frequently renewed, and so being loosened from the tyranny of all useless things thou standest free before Me, and shalt not be confounded. For in that look there is no confusion, nor narrowness, nor doubt, nay, nor even any fear, for in it the soul seeth itself consummated in *Him Who is one*, and perceiveth itself one or one spirit with *the Self-same*, and that Self-same which is God transformed into itself. And thus it worketh all its works in God, nay, thus doth God work His own works in it, so that the soul worketh not so much, as itself is the work of God. Nor from its own weakness doth it leave off this inward deiform movement in any place or at any time, or under any circumstances, however grievous; but it seeth that God hath power over itself in all things, so that it may be an instrument fit and furnished unto the work of God. And thus in truth it knoweth, if things have gone right with it, that God seeth by the eyes of its body, and speaketh by its mouth, and heareth by its ears, and so through the other offices of the body, proceedeth chastely unto all things. And thus is fulfilled that saying of Isaias: "All our works, O Lord, hast Thou wrought for us."* So that in all things nothing is left for man to boast concerning himself, either concerning his own virtue, or his own operation, but all his glorying is in the wholeness of God, and that the only thing which belongs to himself is nothing. By this means he becometh wholly lost in himself, and cannot in any way find himself, but in God he findeth himself whole, in Whom he dwelleth with enough of quietness and security. And for this he exulteth greatly, namely, that all occasion hath been taken from him of glorying in himself, that "God may be all in all."† And in that he thus stands he needeth no glory or praise, for he is full, and the plenitude of God Himself is in him. But wheresoever he desireth glory, there he is convinced that he is altogether empty and without glory, for nowhere doth he seek anything, save where he is vain or empty. Thus it behoveth a man to be ever weak in himself, and to be strong in

---

* Isai. xxvi. 12.   † I. Cor. xv. 28.

our Lord, and frequently to give all things for all, if he will not be straitened; because whatever he keepeth for himself and for his own possession, he is convinced that for this he hath sold God, since God giveth all gifts for the one gift, which is Himself, in order that He may become all ours, and that we be henceforth in no wise beggars, but full.

Chapter XI.

How the interior look of a man becometh clear and enlightened, and his exterior innocent and simple, and how the whole man is made deiform.

IT is not enough to know by estimation merely, but we must know by experience that the soul looketh upon Him Who looketh at all things past, present and to come at one glance, and that He thus speaketh to the soul: "Behold, all thy ways are in My sight, howsoever it may be with thee, whether thou shalt stand before Me and walk with a perfect heart, or whether thou shalt be a wanderer and a fugitive, and shalt vacillate according to every wind of accident. I stand firm and remain without changing. O if thou couldst look upon Me, and see how incommutable is My subsistence, and that in Me there is neither before nor after, but only the self-same, that I alone am: then wouldst thou too be able to be freed from all unevenness and perverse changeableness, and to be with Me in a certain sense the self-same." And this manifestation (on the part of God) is so vehement and strong, that the whole interior of a man, not only of his heart, but even of his body, is marvellously moved and shaken, and faints away in itself, and is quite unable to bear it. And by this means his interior look is made clear without any cloud, and conformable in its own measure to Him, Whom He seeth; and all vanity and all that is alien,* and everything which is

---

* "alietas."

not the self-same, passeth away and vanisheth even as the smoke before a mighty wind. And so too the exterior man is made innocent and simple, and proceedeth with much modesty and gentleness, and humility and pliableness under every circumstance according as necessity requireth of him, that he may be faithful as David, who "went in and out at the king's bidding, and was honourable in his house."* And the whole man is made deiform, so as to be able to look at all things with an equal mind, and never in any way to be disturbed by adverse or grievous circumstances, or to be rendered dissolute by prosperity, but to be frequently renewed by the matured look by which he perceiveth that a consistent evenness is permanently abiding in him, and that he declineth neither to one side nor the other. By this he will accustom himself to be always ready against perplexity or distractions arising from any unforeseen or sudden cause; and if he

---

* I. Kings xxii. 14.

shall do this, then God, Who is exceeding strong, will not suffer that which is deiform within him to be exposed to corporal or spiritual disturbances, or sufferings, or distractions. And inasmuch as he wholly belongs to God, he is on this account consoled concerning everything which may ever happen to him on the part of God, or of the devil, or from the importunities or vexations of man, of whatever kind they may be. He can see too, and hear and call to mind all grievous things, and yet neither be terrified by them nor faint, and this because he possesseth nothing which he can lose, and is certain that God cannot lose what is His own. But how can such great things be entrusted to him who is made anxious and fainteth away in small and daily trials, and who seeketh his own convenience both within and without, even in the least things? Where can such a man freely expose his body and spirit to all grievous trials, present and to come, by denial of himself? Where, in a word, can he have that pure and naked look of unchangeable truth, by which he can see into all things, who is so busied in everything else, even although it be not evil, by the working of his thought or imagination, and by the entanglement and intricate perplexity of his mind, as not to be able,—I do not say when he is much troubled or busied with divers duties, but even during the Divine Office itself, when most of all he ought to be intent upon devotion,—to fix his eyes upon that only Unity in which are all things. If he suffer from such images and thoughts at a season of rest, when he hath time and place and quiet, and other things besides, to help him in watching over his interior, what will he do in the midst of troubles, and when burdened with divers duties? If in anything that happeneth to him his mind vacillateth; if there he falls, where he ought to lift others up; if he setteth his own convenience before his neighbours' need; if in these and like things he fainteth and hath no power over himself, but is held fast under the power of others, then indeed an exceeding thick veil is hung up between him and God, and in no wise is he strong enough to enter into the Holy of Holies, nay, nor even to look into it. And if he communicateth outwardly in the Holy and Divine Mysteries, yet is it only invisibly and without allowing him a share therein, that the Divine equality passeth before him, even that Highest Good, which is given to the soul in proportion to its perfection. And what is more wonderful still, he standeth in the midst of these mysteries and handleth them, but with great dryness, and in a certain way without looking at that which is hidden beneath them, and for the sake of which they exist. And empty and fasting he goeth away from the full table at which frequently he outwardly standeth.

Chapter XII.

Of the hidden sweetness of the spiritual cross, and what it is to persevere therein, and what a man ought to know concerning it.

"BE zealous," with most burning zeal, "for the better gifts" of the spirit.* It is not enough that a man be not much given to vain and useless things, but he ought also to be strong and fervent, so as day and night to faint not in doing good, and to "*rejoice as a giant to run the race*"† of the Lord with boldness, and lovingly to grasp at the struggle held out before him, that is to say, the cross of the Lord. For all our life is and ought to be a cross, and how sweet it is, only he knoweth who feeleth it, for it is so sweet

---

* I. Cor. xii. 31.   † Ps. xviii. 6.

and full of pleasantness and security, this cross of ours, that he who truly loveth it if he fall away from it even but a very little, shall feel much bitterness and great straits. For what good is there which is not in the cross, since therein is the length and breadth and height and depth of all things that can be desired with purity of intention. And since these things are found therein, wheresoever a man may wish to go, he will find space, if only he remain therein; but if he fall away from it, on all sides will he be straitened. And whosoever shall not carefully study to abide continually in the cross of the Lord, falleth away in some slight degree from it, and what is worse, perceiveth not the bitterness of falling away therefrom, because he hath not known the sweetness of permanently abiding therein. Moreover, he falleth away from it as often as he shall fix his eyes on vanities, which estrange him from God, for this is an abomination before the Lord; as often as moved by weariness in well doing he shall fail in that which is his duty; as often as he shall be constrained by any strange fear whatsoever, and lastly, as often as he undergoeth pain and troubles, or as self-seeking worketh in him. But to persevere in the cross is at all times and in every place, under all circumstances, in prosperity or in adversity, and in all things which may come upon him, to strive to preserve evenness of mind; in all things inward or outward, temporal or eternal, thoroughly to abstain from self-seeking, and so to die in the Lord. So also to persevere in the cross is to take no rest, even in the true and needful exultation of the Holy Ghost, as if it were our own, and to embrace nothing at all, within or without, which might pass into our own property, or which tendeth to self-seeking, that in all things which may happen, justly or unjustly, in the sight of all men or in private, no sound of murmur may be heard, and that there may be no alteration nor shaking of the mind, nor lastly, any darkening of the interior look by reason of outward accidents; but that the mind with a good and thorough consciousness of its own state, and with a silent heart, and an equal, humble, and peaceful look, may preserve patience, so that nothing may happen to it unprepared. Convenience and inconvenience from one point of view are held for the same thing, because neither in the one is it made dissolute, nor by the other is it straitened; but because it knoweth and feeleth that it is naturally inclined to convenience and its own quiet, on this account it goeth to meet that inclination, and desireth the more to exercise itself in what is contrary to nature and inconvenient, and so much the more, as it knows that thereby all selfishness is excluded. This is the straight way of the Lord, full of security and glory in the soul, and free from all error, so that every soul that shall not be therein, will be full of anxiety, and of useless fear, and of various doubts, and of dread of destruction from without, and of aversion from our Lord. Yet if a man love the cross of our Lord simply because great security, liberty, and breadth are to be found therein, he doth not love it sincerely, and in this very thing falleth away from it. But when a man living in the cross shall have resigned himself wholly to our Lord and is all His, God in a certain manner wholly resigneth Himself to him, and becometh all his, and the man is made full and wanteth for nothing, neither desireth anything. Behold what a change! But if only for the sake of this change he shall have resigned himself and studied to please God, then is his conduct neither pure nor right, but narrow and impure, and in this respect it is to have fallen away to a very great degree from the cross. Moreover, although a man seem to be in a manner dead to all things, yet ought he, by laying open his whole self to all things, the least as well as the greatest, to proceed according to what every circumstance may require and truth may show; so as even with regard to the conveniences of the body, and its necessities, sleep for instance, rest after fatigue, refreshment, and other such like things, to proceed with such purity and simplicity of intention that he may have no cause to be confounded before his Lord. Should any grievous thing happen unto him, no matter of what kind it be, he will remember that he is on the cross of his Lord, and that nothing else is due to him, nor will he desire aught else but the cross; and so far must the cross needs be grievous unto him and troublesome, as with his whole heart he shall have desired and carried it. But if in certain bodily matters he suffer want (either because he hath not received them from his Lord, and yet if he have them he will not be more happy, and if he have them not he will not be less happy) in no wise is it his Lord's will that he be straitened on this account, or that he should think that he will be less happy by reason of this, even if he should see certain men take it as a grievance and a trouble, and look upon him with a less favourable eye; nor should he wonder at this, for truth suffereth from those who speak against it, how much more then our infirmity? Nor is it possible for one man to please and give satisfaction to all, any more than even the most perfect conversation of our Lord Jesus Christ in the Flesh: always however making exception for humble amendment in the aforesaid, and if he shall not have omitted to do what in him lay. He whose conversation shall thus be in the cross of his Lord, in no wise can be terrified by adversity, whether by day or night, nay, not even were it to last for ever, since he feels himself ready to undergo all things whatsoever, which may happen to the honour of his Lord by His disposal or permission. For if he truly loveth justice, then in whatever way God may think fit to punish and correct his excesses and his turning away from Him, nothing else but this can he desire; nay, if God should wish him to be in purgatory, even this also he will desire, in order that whatever hath been done in him contrary to justice and to truth, may be purged away.* So also both to die and

---

* A little further on, chapter xvi. the writer pushes this assertion, so far as to seem to go beyond the boundary line of sound doc-

to live, in some sort, he holdeth for the same thing, nor is he saddened by the departure of any thing, because he took not any excessive joy or rest at its coming. For what is there that can come to him as comfort, who enjoyeth the Highest Good and Very Blessedness, which is God, and who is not increased nor lessened by mere accidents? Of a truth this Blessedness hath nothing in common with accidents, so that he who is blessed with it, even were all conveniences to come to him, would be no more blessed, and if all were to depart from him would be no less blessed. And although all this sounds wonderful to the ear, yet indeed is there no presumption in feeling this, because it is not on the surface, but cometh from a profound union and conformity with God, nor can the stranger, that is the carnal man, in any way attain to this, for great injustice hath rule over him; nay, even if he have much confidence, yet is this wholly

---

trine. See note at chapter xvi., where, however, it will be found that the passage in question has been tampered with.—*Trans.*

vain, unless it shall proceed from union with God and in consequence of the reformation of his soul. But perchance a man may say that "we ought not to be more wise than it behoveth to be wise, but to be wise unto sobriety."* This is true, but what is it in which we ought to be wise? Is it not in this, that we have been "created unto the likeness and image of God," and that we "may be perfect, even as our Father in heaven is perfect?"† Think ye that it is the will of our Lord Jesus Christ, Who prayed to the Father for us, that we might be one, as He is in the Father, and the Father in Him, and that being perfected together in one, we might know that the Father hath loved us, as He hath loved the Son,‡ and Who prayed for many other like graces; think ye that it is the will of our Lord Jesus Christ that we should be wanderers from our Father and strangers to Him? So also of inward certainty the Blessed Peter

---

* Rom. xii. 3. † Matt. v. 48.
‡ John xvii. 11, 26.

The Fiery Soliloquy with God. 41

saith: "Labour the more, that by good works ye may make your calling and election sure."* If this and such like wisdom is to be wise in opposition to God, then is God altogether in opposition to Himself, for it is nothing else, but in all things, inwardly and outwardly, in time and in eternity, to be at the beck of God, and to be subject to His will; and that in us there should be no dissimilitude which might offend the eyes of God's goodness, so that self (inasmuch as it is self) be nothing, but God all in all: yet, that self in God and with God (so far as this is possible) may be everything. But what if "*the judgments of God are a great deep*"?† A great deep indeed, and moreover also a "*man knoweth not whether he be worthy of love or hatred.*"‡ Nevertheless what is His own God cannot lose, for He can do nought against Himself: for if He shall have united a man unto Himself, and this man is in a certain manner (made partaker

---

* II. Pet. i. 10.

† Ps. xxxv. 7.   ‡ Eccl. ix. 1.

of) what God is, justice, namely, and power, and truth and equity, will not God love Himself? For how could the Prophet say in his exultation: "Thy judgments shall help me; Thy judgments are delightful; I was mindful, O Lord, of Thy judgments of old, and I was comforted, and in Thy judgments have I hoped exceedingly,"* and many other such words, if he had not wholly fallen away from himself, that is to say as to vices, and been made in a certain way justice† in the region of similitude, so to speak, holding it for most certain that God could not damn him? But there is also another region in the soul, the region, namely, of dissimilitude, full of snares and chains, and tribulations, and groans, and straits, and in it there are thorns, and exceeding great depression, and destruction, and confusion, and opposition, all of which arise from the thought of our own weakness, as well as from the manifold defect of the inward

---

* Ps. cxviii.

† II. Cor. v. 21. "*Ut nos efficeremur justitia Dei in ipso.*"

and outward man, which is daily felt and experienced* more than it behoveth. In this region, thorns and thistles and briers grow copiously and abundantly, in one man more, in another less, yet so that hardly any man can be free from these useless weeds. In this region it is that we must ask with the Prophet David: "Enter not into judgment with Thy servant, O Lord; Lord, reprove me not in Thy wrath; O forsake me not, for I am afraid of Thy judgments!"†

---

* *Sentitur et experitur.* Deponent verbs have often a passive signification in the works of Mediæval writers. Thus Alb. Mag. de Adhær. Deo, c. 14, sed nec velis revereri ab aliis, allisque præferri. Cæsar. Dial. Mir. v. 4, de violentia in discipulum facta a magistro conqueritur, ab adversario respondetur.—Suso. Horol. Æt. Sap. i. 6, experiri potest, fari non potest.

† Ps. vi. 2; cxviii. 120; cxlii. 2.

Chapter XIII.

How interior vices, together with the devil their chief, never cease to lay snares for the soul that loveth God.

IT happeneth at times when the crowd of vices, and manifold impediments, and strange causes and attacks are endeavouring to get the mastery in the upper region of the soul, that they make a boast and say reproachfully: "Where is thy God? Where is thy kingdom and the guardian thereof? Lo! it is we who reign and have dominion, not only on thy earth, but even in thy heaven, and we are no longer driven out, as we were wont to be, by that pure, bare, and mature look, before which we were unable to stand, for now it is exceedingly clouded over by us, and yieldeth easily to any little object. Nor have we much care about the graver things that have to be done, provided that in those that are of least moment it be hampered; that is to say, by strange and restless occupation, and that it be content with the straits in which it is straitened by us. And although it hath no great leaning towards us, yet is it rendered inapt and lukewarm, and is led by custom without any great fervour to perform the duties which have to be done. But oh! that this of which we boast might only last, for we fear lest a stronger than we should come upon us and cast us out, and keep us out for good, so that no longer could we enter, nay, nor even dare to come near the place where once we were secure, but now dwell in dread; for it seemeth unto us that the Lord will fight for this man against us. And although he has been oppressed by us, yet see how his groans and the deep sighs of his heart, and the tear-drops of his eyes, those not only of his inward but also of his outward eyes, seem to mount up to the Lord, Who hath even now determined to free him from his manifold servitude, and to restore him to his old liberty; and if he shall obtain this again for himself, he will vehemently oppress and reproach us, so that we shall not dare even to appear before him. We ask of Thee, therefore, O Lord, that if Thou castest us out, Thou wouldst leave unto us at least a little secret doorway, so that if peradventure Thou shouldst leave him for a little while, we may boast ourselves of our former dominion over him. And if Thou wilt not do this, then at least let that beggar, or whatever he may be called, know that as long as there is breath in him we will not cease day or night to attack him; we will multiply snares for him, so that wherever he turn he may find himself caught at least for a little while; we will anticipate his vigils, so that if peradventure his eyes shall not be fixed upon the Lord at dawn, we will be beforehand with him, and take possession of his mind. We will tell him all kinds of fables, and we will place before him divers images, especially at the Divine Office, as often as he shall not have considered how he should love the law of his Lord, and how he should appear in His Presence, and before His *open face*,* for to this we frequently call. And we know how to prepare snares wherein to deceive him; for what we cannot do of ourselves, that we will endeavour to do by means of others and by those who are in a certain way familiar with him, so that he may suspect nothing sinister. For who is he, that he can escape our hands through everything and in everything? Many and great are they whom we have cast down; in no wise then let us despair of this poor little beggar, who thinketh himself to be somewhat, and yet who lieth beneath the feet of those who once were very eminent and enlightened."

Then the Lord, when He seeth this vehement conflict between various temptations and obstacles, and that the man is left to himself, and when He considereth his groans and his labour, and the boasting of his adversaries, what doth the Lord say to this? "I am in My holy

---

* II. Cor. iii. 18.

temple," saith the Lord, " let all the earth keep silent before My Face,"* and strange boasting, let it not so much as even appear. Know ye not that I am the guardian of My own kingdom ? And if for a short moment I left the man to himself, in order to prove whether peradventure he would be found faithful and stable, as indeed he hath been found, think ye that I was not present, although I was hidden ? For although ye have vehemently attacked him, yet did he ever trust in Me, nor did he join himself to you. In vain therefore have ye boasted, and behold, ye stand not, nay, ye have " never stood in the truth, because the truth is not in you."† As I live, shall ye not be driven out of My kingdom for ever, and behold now ye fear, and why ? Is it not because ye are vain, for fear never cometh, save where there is no truth. In a word, ye have threatened to attack him cruelly, and to multiply your snares for him, as long as he shall live, so that

---

* Habac. ii. 20.   † John viii. 44.

peradventure he may fall and be taken, as ye have already taken many. And this indeed is true enough, but why did they fall? Because they stood not in the truth, for they were found in themselves and not in Me. But to this man I say: "*Take courage and be strong*,"* and faint not in thy labours. As yet indeed there still remain many conflicts, and many temptations, and many an utter forsaking, and tribulations day and night even to the last moment, when thy soul shall go out of thy body; but fear not before their face, act like a man, and finish thy course, for it is short, nor suffer thyself in any wise to grow weary in what thou hast to do. Whensoever they shall have dominion over thee, if thou shalt stand before Me in the truth, and in simplicity, and shalt walk before Me in the sincerity of thy heart,† if in all that thou hast to do or not to do thou shalt fix thy gaze on Me, if, in a word, thou shalt place all thy care and solicitude, and hope, and strength, and

---

* Jos. i. 6.   † II. Cor. i. 12.

glory in Me, and shalt glory in nothing at all, save in My cross, if thou shalt deny and wholly lose thyself, then wholly and in all fulness shalt thou be found in Me, nor will there be cause for thee to fear. For in Me thine adversaries shall not seek thee, but if in thyself they shall find thee, then indeed will there come attacks, and doubts, and fear lest peradventure thou mayest be overcome. Let them be multiplied then who trouble thee within and without; only do thou place thyself near to Me and take refuge with Me, and thou shalt have no fear of all the robber-bands that shall fight against thee, for "*I will hide thee in the secret place of My Face*,"[*] so that thou shalt not be found by any stranger. Thou art indeed in the midst of snares, and amongst many enemies, but under My shadow shalt thou live amongst them, until I shall call thee. And if I delay, prepare thy soul and wait for Me, and ever remember to offer Thyself unto Me as a sacrifice well-pleasing in My sight.

---

[*] Ps. xxx. 21.

Chapter XIV.

That the interior man, both in the presence and in the absence of grace, maketh profit and increase, and how he is taught by the Angels in what way he should stand in the Presence of God.

"COME unto Him, and be enlightened, and your face shall not be confounded."* And who shall be able to stand, Lord Jesus, before Thy open face? For frequently dost Thou exhort me to stand before Thee, and look upon Thee. And how shall I be able to do this, unless Thou shalt take away the too thick veil which is hung up between me and Thee? For although on the one hand I shall rest in Thee, standing in Thy Presence without being confounded, and having all

---

* Ps. xxxiii. 6.

things in common with Thee, yet on the other hand am I mindful and conscious of my own weakness, and how unlike I am to Thee, and then am I shaken with exceeding great fear. On the one hand Thou sayest unto me: "*My Son, all that I have is thine*,"* and see how the heavens and the earth are full of My glory. Then, on the other hand, Thou sayest: "*What fellowship hath light with darkness?*" and what communion is there between truth and vanity? But oh! that that might first get the victory which cometh last, and that "*that which is mortal might be swallowed up by life*,"† vanity by truth, darkness by light. Yet however it may be, through Thee I will surmount all difficulties, and more than ever fix my eyes on Thee. And if, when I see somewhat of Thee, and this only through a veil, I so vehemently exult, and my eyes fail in the brightness of Thy Wisdom, what would happen unto me wert Thou openly to show to me Thyself? But when will this

---

* Luke xv. 31. † II. Cor. vi. 14.

be? thinkest Thou, Lord, that it will ever be?

Be faithful, it shall be. But when? When I shall call thee; only do thou prepare thy soul and wait for Me, lest peradventure when I come thou be not prepared, and unfit to see Me openly; for with blear and weak eyes thou canst not see Me.

Be it so, then, O Father; Thy will be done, yet will I make complaint to Thee, that often do I experience my own exceeding great wretchedness, in that Thou hidest Thy Face, so that I see Thee not. And were it not that when Thou hidest Thy Face, Thou sufferest some relics as it were of Thyself to remain with me, by which I may receive strength from Thee, straightway would I fall away in doing what then Thou hast sent me to do.

But if I shall delay to reveal Myself, what wilt thou do?

I will wait for Thee, and I will hold converse with my own darkness, and I will say within myself: "*Will God cast me off for ever, will He never be more favourable again? Or will God forget to show mercy? Or will He, in His anger, shut up His mercies?"* Yet will I be faithful to Thee, and I will rejoice in my poverty, nor in any wise will I admit of any consolation, until Thou shalt reveal Thyself; yea, and the tear drops of my eyes, both inward and outward, shall flow more abundantly, until they reach to Thee. And "*my tears shall be my bread day and night*," † until they who trouble me both see and feel that "*Thou art my God and my refuge*," ‡ and that not wholly hast Thou forsaken me, but that by hiding Thy face from me, Thou hast proved me whether I be faithful.

And if wholly I shall forsake thee?

Then, were I to know this for certain, I confess from the very bottom of this heart of mine with which I love Thee, that even then I would do no less day or night, as long as the breath should be in me, than if I were to know for certain that Thou wouldst never be separated from me. Do

---

* Ps. lxxvi. 8, 10.

† Ps. xli. 4.   ‡ Ps. xv. 2; xxx. 4.

therefore whatsoever shall seem right and pleasing in Thy sight; in Thy hands I am both as to my body and my spirit; wheresoever I shall go, there will I praise Thee, and exult exceedingly, and if not everywhere in Thy mercy, yet at least in Thy justice; and whatsoever I shall know to be pleasing in Thy sight, that will I strive after. Lay therefore Thy salve upon me, of whatsoever kind it may be, grievous or light, wheresoever Thou knowest there are wounds, especially in my eyes: willingly will I bear them for Thy sake: only may I be cured that I may be made fit to see Thee. And yet, who shall console me, when Thou goest from me? Straightway even when I look not for them, there come to meet me divers little consolations, nay, rather little desolations; but all these are burdensome to me, for in some poor little way have I experienced how sweet is Thy Cross, and so to fall away from it, even ever so little, is to me a bitterness and a desolation. So also I would rather suffer bitter tribulation and die, than knowingly admit of comfort from other things, from what source soever it may come. And if at times it happeneth that such comfort should creep over my soul, from want of care on my part, peradventure, or from too little love for Thee, yet doth it bring to me no rest in Thee. And lo! they who love Thee and look upon Thee without hindrance say unto me: "Why dost thou stand so frequently looking up into heaven? Why dost thou gaze and sigh after Him '*Who dwelleth in light inaccessible;*'* for this is He Who '*hath made darkness His covert, and the clouds His chariot*'?"† And although "*clouds and thick darkness be round about Him,*" yet *justice* and *judgment*, and to walk holily in the truth, are the foundation and *preparation of His Throne,*‡ if the soul is to look upon His open face, and He Himself is to be seen in the soul as on His throne. This is He "*before Whose Face the mountains melt like wax,*"§ nay, not only the mountains, but the heavens and the earth,

---

* I. Tim. vi. 16.   † Ps. xvii. 12; ciii. 3.
‡ Ps. lxxxviii. 15.   § Ps. xcvi. 5.

and all that in them is, and the very soul itself, all melt away and are dissolved before His open Face, as thou thyself wilt be able to experience and feel, when thou shalt stand in His presence to contemplate Him. Consider therefore first: how thou oughtest to stand in His sight, and with how pure a love He ought to be loved, and that with a gaze purified from all defects He ought to be looked upon. In the second place, and above all, let it not be with blear but sound eyes that thou lookest upon His glorious Face, and see whether it be not true that all things melt away before His Face, and that thou thyself too meltest away together with them; and point out unto us also how He appeareth unto thee; for this we desire exceedingly. And if thou wilt listen then we say: "O that thou couldst stand together with us, and recognise how glorious is His Face; then indeed would all other things whatsoever seem unto thee but as nothing. Oh! were it lawful for thee to look into that most deep abyss, not only in the overflowing exultation which ye men enjoy on earth, but in the very origin of thy being and of all beings, *of Whom are all things, and by Whom are all things*, and Who is *God all in all.*"

Behold I am a poor little one, humble and small, more vile than all who live upon the face of the earth, and often is my interior clouded over exceedingly, how then shall I be able to do anything at all, unless He of Whom we speak shall show unto me His Face? For ye exhort me, as if it were in my power, and as if I held myself in my own hands, so that I could present myself free from all form before His countenance, and after having overstepped every obstacle, look upon that Face of His, Who *dwelleth in light inaccessible*, I who am weighed down with the burden of this corruptible body of mine, and who am often found in the region of dissimilitude and of my own darkness, in which I have need, not as one who is rich, to supplicate the Face of my Lord, or as one who is "*upright and pure to dwell with His countenance*,"* but as a poor man to

---
* Ps. cxxxix. 14.

prostrate myself humbly at His feet. Ye tell me next to look upon His Face, as ye look at It, as if I already saw, and were certain that I were free from all strange bondage, and restored by liberty to my pristine origin; and yet, far from doing this, I look upon myself as cast away far down in the deep of my own darkness, and far away from the sight of His eyes, so that at times I hardly dare to look at Him, nay, nor even to so much as lift up my eyes. For what marvel is it, that such as ye are ever looking without ceasing upon His Face, and without ever turning away from It, when ye dwell in a certain sense in the very vestibule of the Most Blessed Trinity, and are hindered by no corporeal objects or images as I am? Neither memory, nor sensible understanding do ye use; nor are ye led up from creatures to look upon and love the Highest Good, but ye stand unchangeable with the Unchangeable; with Him and in Him the Very Good are ye good, being made partakers of His essence, Who is the Very Being of all things. Not indeed that ye can lose the properties of your own essence, and become the Very Being, but ye are united with It, so that not even for a moment are ye torn away from His Countenance. Nor are ye free in this sense: that is to say, as if at divers times ye had been for a certain while the slaves of some vice, as I confess that I am, not without a groan; for so great and so overwhelming are the infirmities to which I am subjected, and by which I am distracted, that for their very multitude they cannot be numbered, so that, wherever I reach, in body or in mind, everywhere do they meet me, although sorely against my will, and in spite of my many struggles; and they cloud the sharpness of my mind with which I am wont to look upon His Face, until the tender Father shall reveal His Face, and hide me in Himself, so that I may not be found by others who are strangers. But for how long all this? Who will grant unto me, if not continually, at least very frequently, to see myself standing before His Face, and walking in the light of His Countenance? Yet however seldom it may be that He shall reveal Himself unto me and I shall look upon Him, I confess not only that all things else vanish away, but also that all the interior of the inward man liquefieth in love and melteth away. For so mighty and vehement is this love, that there hardly remaineth unto me aught of myself, being as if I were wholly helpless and poor; because He requireth of me so many and such great things, that when I have given all that I have and all that I can, yet seem I to have paid Him nothing at all. But in this exceeding poverty, nay, rather in this excess of riches I find nothing healthier or more acceptable to God, than in all things that can happen wholly to resign myself to Him, that He Himself may pay for me what He asketh of me, and that I may not at all be a lover of myself, save only in this, that being united to God, in Him, through Him, and for Him, I may love myself and all things. For it is God's will that I should love myself for the same object for which He loveth me, and not for any other, so that wholly and entirely I may be His, and that I may be transformed into Him. And when I shall thus love God and all things, I love nothing else in me or of me, save my God.

Chapter XV.

That by the love of God true security is infused into a man.

THANKS be to Thee, O my Light, Thou Light Eternal, Thou Light that never faileth, Thou Highest and Incommutable Good, in Whose Presence I, Thy poor and humble little servant stand. Thanks be to Thee, for lo! I see, I see the light shining in the darkness.

And what seest thou in the light?

I see that Thou lovest me exceedingly, and that if I abide in Thee it will be as impossible for Thee not to take care of me at all times and in all places, and in everything that happeneth unto me, as it is impossible for Thee not to care for

Thyself. And Thou givest me Thy whole Self, to be mine whole and undivided, if at least I shall be Thine whole and undivided. And when I shall be thus all Thine, even as from everlasting Thou hast loved Thyself, so from everlasting Thou hast loved me: for this means nothing more than that Thou enjoyest Thyself in me, and that I by Thy grace enjoy Thee in myself, and myself in Thee. And when in Thee I shall love myself, nothing else but Thee do I love, because Thou art in me, and I in Thee, glued together as one and the self-same thing, which henceforth and for ever cannot be divided. And when we men each of us love what is good and virtuous in one another,* this is nothing else but that Thou lovest Thyself. But if I shall abide entirely and wholly in Thee, as it is impossible for Thee to perish, so is it impossible for me to perish. And in this union I have no need to turn away from creatures, however ignoble and unbecom-

---

* Conf. ch. 38.

ing they may seem, since all things have been created very good; but so must I stand in the midst of all creatures as to be inclined towards all without sensuality, and to turn away from all without irksomeness or pain. So also when in this light I look upon myself from the lower part of my soul I see that I am in great and exceeding thick darkness, and I abominate myself, so that I can hardly bear myself. And therein do I suffer the reproaches of my enemies, and of many impediments and useless occupations, by which I am often bound fast and held subject, for continually do they seek to obtain possession of the whole kingdom even in its higher part, boasting at times that they already possess the lower. But lo! as I stand before Thee, in Thyself and not in myself, I hear a voice exceeding terrible, speaking for me, and saying unto those who vex and trouble me: "Come not nigh hither, for the place in which he standeth upright before Me is holy and consecrated ground;* neither

---

* Exod. iii. 5.

have ye any share in him; nay, neither is there anywhere any access for you." But they answer: "What care we, if we cannot reach him there! How long will he stand therein? For of a sudden will he fall headlong down to us into his own familiar darkness, and then we shall gain possession of our accustomed place." But how long, O Lord, shall these enemies of Thine and mine utter reproaches against the temple and throne of Thy glory? *How long shall I take counsels in my soul,** day and night against one thing and another, that at length they may all alike be cast down, nor seek to rise again? Lo! one saith: "I will reign;" and another, "Nay, but I reign;" and a third, "it is I who will first possess this region." Every depraved and false imagination desireth to have place and power in Thy kingdom. I beseech Thee, therefore, O Lord, that this accursed Dagon† which hath been set up close to the Ark of Thy Eternal Testament, and (what is worse)

---

* Ps. xli. 2.   † I. Kings v. 4.

at times even above the Ark, may fall wholly down upon its face, and its strength having been cut off, may not come to itself again, so as to be restored anew to its former place. Let all the idols of sins and vices, I beseech Thee, be cast down from the throne of Thy glory, that Thou alone mayest reign thereon, and that I may be no more wretchedly unstable, and a runaway from Thee.

Chapter XVI.

That to love justice and truth, and in all things to seek the glory of God, is to abide in the cross of our Lord.

HE who truly is on the cross of our Lord, and embraceth the cross, he it is who loveth justice and truth, and seeketh not his own convenience, or honour, or glory, either now or for ever, but at all times and in every place, the glory of God. It followeth therefore, if it be for the greater honour and glory of

The Fiery Soliloquy with God. 67

God, that he should be in the depths of hell for ever, rather than in the eternal glory of God and of His Angels, that being such, in nothing. is he able to desire aught else, nor inwardly to feel either opposition or repugnance.* And if this

---

* This passage seems to border upon some of the sixty-eight propositions condemned by Innocent XI. in 1687, as well as upon some of the twenty-three condemned by Innocent XII. in 1689; perhaps also upon one of Ekkard's propositions condemned by John XXII. in 1329. The force of the passage has been even intensified by the addition of the word "*debere*" but this, as Strange points out in his edition of the "Soliloquy," has evidently been made by a later hand. The word has clearly been foisted into the sentence, where it is out of place. It is therefore omitted in the translation. In defence of the holy writer it may be observed that the "Fiery Soliloquy" has never been accused of contradicting any point of the Catholic faith. In 1613 it was approved as "worthy to be read and studied by every Christian, and as marvellously calculated to point out a certain path to the highest perfection." Again, in 1616, it was approved of at Cologne as containing nothing contrary either to Catholic faith or morals; and once more in 1849 it received the "Imprimatur" of the Vicar General of Cologne. Further, it may be said that the case contemplated by the holy writer is one of abstract impossibility, for of course it could never be for the greater honour and glory of God that any soul that truly loves Him, should be for ever in hell, rather than in eternal glory. May not the passage therefore be rather classed with those yearnings of Divine love, and passionate declarations of submission to His holy Will, which led S. Paul to desire to be an anathema from Christ for his

is so, nay, because it is so in great and deep matters, how much more will it be so in matters of least moment, and in the circumstances and events of every day, that is to say, in heaviness or irksomeness, or weariness, or pain of body or soul, which happen of a certainty by the disposition of God? Therefore ought the soul entirely and wholly to be stripped of self-seeking, and to be united in all things to the Will of God and to His disposal, and not to shift about according to every wind of accident, here and there. For if it

---

brethren, and our own S. Anselm to declare that "he would rather be in hell if he were pure of sin, than possess the kingdom of heaven under the pollution of sin"? To bring one's self into such a state as to be utterly indifferent to one's own salvation, and to fear nothing not even hell, as the Quietists taught, is one thing;—for a Saint or Servant of God to declare in a soliloquy with God, that if by an impossibility his damnation should be for God's greater glory, God's will is his will, is surely quite another, although no doubt such declarations of early mystics have been sometimes misunderstood or even perverted by later mystical writers, and are rather to be wondered at than imitated. For information, easily accessible to all, upon the errors of the Quietists and Semi-Quietists see Alban Butler's note to the Life of S. John of the Cross, November 24, which is also quoted by F. Guy, in his edition of Hilton's Scale of Perfection (Richardson and Son).—*Trans.*

shall lean upon what is accidental, and suffer itself to be drawn to this or that side according to its choice and convenience, then in truth it hath not, neither feeleth that only *One and the Self-same*, for Whom are all things.

Chapter XVII.

That the soul, free from everything belonging to itself, is everywhere secure in God.

A TRAVELLER without incumbrances walketh everywhere in safety. If thou hast Me, saith the Truth Itself, what more dost thou require? What is wanting to thee, or what is there in Me that is displeasing unto thee, that thou shouldst care for other things which are caused or happen to thee from without, for in whatsoever way they shall happen they can add nothing to thee, nor take aught from thee? Dost thou seek to be made blessed on thy journey towards heaven? Why, dost not thou weigh the matter more deeply with thyself, that thou art on thy pilgrimage, nay, even banished in exile, and bound by many fetters, and subject to many a strange kind of servitude? Call to mind whatsoever thou wilt of the things that are outside, if thou shalt be united to Me, and faithful to Me, and familiar from within, in nothing can they hinder thee, and in nothing can they help thee, in what way soever they shall happen. Be therefore even as one who goeth on his journey, free and all-unburdened and unbound by any fastening whatsoever, whether outward or inward, in the upper region of thy soul. And if thus thou shalt be, everywhere at all times and under all circumstances shalt thou walk secure; for thou hast nothing that thou canst lose. But if thou hast anything and possessest it as thine own, not only of external goods, but also of those which are internal and spiritual, deservedly dost thou fear to lose it, because it is put in a public and unsafe place, where thy enemies can come and snatch it from thee.

But if thou shalt be all poor and naked, then I will be thy riches and thy ornament, thy glory and thy strength, and nothing hast thou to doubt, for I cannot lose Myself. In all things, therefore, that are to be done outside, do diligently and cheerfully day and night what is in thee, and beyond that rest wholly satisfied; for nothing can happen so miserable, so evil, so desperate, so abject, nor in those things that are outside can any accidents occur of so grave a nature but that ever there will remain within thee the highest counsel, stable, firm, and incommutable, to which it seemeth but a little matter in what way soever the things that are outside may happen to thee, whether in this wise or otherwise, in all accidental circumstances. For what if this or that shall happen of all the things that thou canst think of? Am not I thy life, and am not I alive? Thinkest thou that I pass away with accidents, and am shaken to and fro as thou art? Behold! I am all thine, what more dost thou desire? And if thou hast Me, am I not all things to thee?

Why then dost thou not abide stable in Me, enjoying Me the Highest, Incommutable and Most Excellent Good, for Whom thou wert created? Have not I promised thee that I will have care of thee in all things that may happen unto thee? And that I will be with thee wheresoever thou shalt go, if thou shalt be faithful unto Me? And if I shall be thy life, as indeed I am, thou canst well be without all things, and yet suffer no harm unto thyself. Shall not all things forsake thee? And if thou shalt lean upon them thou wilt remain wretched and desolate. And if all things shall happen according to thy wish, and if in all that is outside thou shalt be successful, yet nought of confidence or security can this bestow upon thee in the hour of death, should I be left out or absent.

Chapter XVIII.

Of the exercise of the spiritual man, especially of the Religious in the Divine Office.

AT all times, and in every place, and under all circumstances, and most of all and in a special manner at the Divine Office will I stand before the Lord, whole and entire, with a most humble heart and body, lovingly subject to the whole world even as if I were the dust of men's feet, fleeing like some little child, or some poor little lamb, or some lonely wandering chicken, beneath the care and under the wings of our Lord Jesus. Then too very reverently will I converse before His face with *open face*,* with my mind unshaken, unconfused, and quiet, and with counsel well digested, and with seriousness both inwardly and outwardly. In-

---
* I. Cor. iii. 18.

wardly, against hurtful subjection to aught else but to Him, whether this shall come from human respect or fear, convenience or inconvenience. Outwardly against softness, instability, over-vain occupations and sensual distractions. And so with my soul reformed, and a perfect mind, will I follow up the meaning and understanding of the Holy Scriptures and of the Sacraments. By my memory : that is to say by avoiding whatever differeth from it or is obscure, or is not suitable thereto, by always going forward with evenness of mind and with sincerity, and by stripping myself speedily of every strange anxiety and vicious affection, so that whatever may come into my memory of all that is done, or can be done, on any side whatsoever, my soul (without care about itself, but wholly resigned to God, and consoled as to all things else,) on the one hand may in no wise suffer harm so as to be moved either by what is little or what is great, nor on the other hand may be depressed so as to fear whatever may be grievous or irksome.

In the second place by my reason; that is to say, by speedily and freely following after the Eternal Wisdom Itself, the Incommutable Truth, Justice, Equity, and Peace, so as to see how they proceed outwardly to all creatures, looking at, and accepting all things that are or can be made in truth and wisdom, that is, as they are, and not otherwise. Lastly, by my reformed will, that is to say, by earnestly and eagerly going forth to do all that I have to do. Let my soul strive day by day to make progress in God, to fall away from itself, and wholly to lose itself, so that in no wise it may be able to find itself, but that it may come into deep self-annihilation or self-abjection, so as to die to itself and all things in God, and to live on God, working all things through Him.

Chapter XIX.

That nothing is sweeter or more glorious than for the soul to inhere in the Highest Good, and to become conformed to the Holy Trinity.

AFTER keen examination and diligent discussion of all things, nothing do I feel more sweet or glorious or well-pleasing to God, and more full of all glory and exultation, or more rich and abundant in all good things, than for the soul fully to unite itself to the Highest and Incommutable Good, which standeth ever immoveable from everlasting, and which no accidents can reach, for It needeth not either time or place; and so to be brought back to its original conformity, and to become one with Unity itself, that is to say, with God. For as God, Who is the Highest Good, is Virtue, Truth, Justice,

Eternal Wisdom, ever remaining what He is, enjoying Himself in all things, and loving Himself: so too the soul, being made partaker of what God is, overaboundeth with exultation and joy in all things. It standeth and passeth on, and proceedeth with God and in God: so much the greater in God as it is less in itself, because in all things it hath forgotten itself and passed on into God. And it is clothed with the light of the Eternal Wisdom as with a garment, and it is surrounded on all sides by truth and equity, as by an impregnable shield, and it is set on fire with the glow of charity. For as heated iron is made all fire, so the soul united with Love is made all love, save only its own essential properties, which must needs be different for ever. Therefore it is that the soul united with God, whatever is to be done, ought to do it wholly through God and in God, and frequently to look at the Truth, the Eternal Wisdom, Justice, and the Highest Good, to see how they look at all things, at what is like and unlike, equal and unequal, good and evil, at what is within and what is without, and yet notwithstanding stand immutable. So also ought the soul to strive by much endeavour, in its own measure, to become one with their look; and to forget itself, so far as may be. And this look is immense, not bounded on any side, and so vehement and mighty, keen and strong is it, that no power and nothing strange can subsist before it, for whatever is not truth, or in the truth is vanity, and vanity hath never stood, nor can stand before the face of truth. And thus the soul becometh conformed to the Holy Trinity, in its own measure, by the three powers which it possesseth. First, it is like unto the Eternal Father, Who is without beginning and from none by its memory, which in a certain way containeth and retaineth all things, and from it all things proceed. And by it the soul becometh so conformed, if it be naked and free from all strange forms, that can transform it, as never to suffer in any wise from fantasies, but powerfully to operate in all things, and wholly to disdain that its own nobleness should be busied about what is exceeding vile. Secondly, it is like unto the Son, Who is Truth Itself, and Eternal Wisdom, by its reason, through which it becometh conformed, if in all things it shall walk in the sight of Truth, and if all things temporal or eternal, inward or outward, equal or unequal, and all things that are made or done taste unto it, as they are: and if this be so, then not in anything can it be straitened. Thirdly, it is like unto the Holy Ghost, by its will, through which it becometh conformed to Him, if when the memory receiveth nothing strange or useless, the reason or the understanding receiveth nothing save what is good, true and just. By the will is it moved with its whole affection, and vehemently desireth what the memory and reason judge ought to be willed and loved. And this is that true beatitude of soul, which as much the nearer, more perfect, and more conformed it is to God in this present time, will be so much the more pleasing unto God, and nearer unto Him in the full consummation of beatitude. If, moreover, we speak of the large and broad effluence into that Immensity, in which are the aforesaid which are ascribed to God, Truth, namely, Peace, Charity, and the rest, in no wise can they not love and enjoy themselves. Here, however, there is no question of those things that are outside, that is to say, how they happen, in this way or that way, for or against, according to what we hope for or against our hope, for none of these affect the soul in its higher conformity and reformation. And although we must needs be involved in many and divers accidents, as long as we live here, yet diligently ought we to take care, lest they reach the higher part of the soul, as in the case of the disposal of property, anxiety about the way in which it is to be made, the administration of all things that relate to what is without. Yet let also Martha remain in the lower place, let her be careful, and troubled about many things, if it must needs be. But to the one only thing that is necessary let Mary cleave, let her busy herself with the Word

Eternal, with justice, wisdom, truth, so that in one and the same man both lives, each in its own state, may be practised and perfected.

Chapter XX.

How to a devout man his highest good is to be with God, and his greatest evil to be without God.

"I AM straitened on every side,"* and conflicts and troubles beset me, unless frequently with very great diligence and care I converse inwardly before the Face of God, to be with which is my highest good, and to be without which my highest evil. And if I persevere therein, then at least at times I may be allowed to see light with light,† that is to say wisdom, in which all things may taste

---

* Dan. xiii. 22.
† Ps. xxxv. 10, "in lumine tuo videbimus lumen."

unto me as they are, and the naked truth in itself, in which I may be able to have truth concerning all things. First concerning myself, namely, that I am a pure simple nothing, and that what is in me, of myself is nothing, save that according to the truth it ought to be despised and trampled upon by every creature. And thus set up, as it were wholly outside myself, looking at myself from afar off, and despising myself, I will go forth together with the naked truth of all things that are, in height and depth, and length and breadth, according to the measure in which that truth proceedeth forth to all things, looking at what is unequal with equal gaze, and at what is full of tumult with peacefulness.

Chapter XXI.

The prayer of a man, whose soul is clouded, for the illumination of his heart.

O INCOMMUTABLE Truth, Thou art the Light of my eyes; O Eternal Wisdom, Justice, Peace, Thou art all my good, and strength, and my praise, with which I run in latitude, and without which I am straitened on every side exceedingly. I, Thy little child, Thy poor little servant, useless within and without, the least of all in my Father's house, behold I kneel down in heart and body, and salute Thee from afar off, for I am not clean enough to be fixed in Thee. Take away the veil, purify my face, that I may see Thee clearly, and that the darkness of my heart may flee away, so that my soul may joy and exult in Thy Divine Light, and run quickly on her path, and in sweet jubilee praise and exalt Thy Name.

And who shall be able to follow Thee, O Lord Jesus, whithersoever Thou goest? Who amongst men shall be able to follow after that Eternal Wisdom "*which reacheth mightily from end to end, and ordereth all things sweetly?*"* And behold! because of this as I stand before Thy Face, the tears of my heart and body flow up to Thee, for hardly after all is it granted unto me, at least for a little while to be able to follow Thee, so bound am I and fettered by my very self. Oh! wilt Thou contain Thyself with regard to this, and not rather visit me with the arm of Thy might, and have pity upon the fetters and hindrances by which I am bound and straitened, so as to restore me to my former position close to Thee, and that I may no longer belong to any one else, nor even to myself, but that I may be wholly Thine alone?

"So far," saith the Truth, "wilt thou be able to follow Me, as thou shalt have gone away from Thyself. Do therefore

---

* Wisd. viii. 1.

whatsoever thou mayest, thy outward troubles will not cease, thy inward trials will not be quieted, until thou shalt be all changed into Me, and shalt fall away wholly from thyself. What, thinkest thou, is the reason why the voice of the turtle* is not heard more frequently in our land of the living? Peradventure, because thou art no true and desolate turtle, and because thou hast as yet a mate and a lover in the land of the sorrowing. For the voice of the true and the chaste turtle, whose voice is sweet, and whose face is fair, is frequently heard in our land."

Chapter XXII.

That he who is truly poor in spirit should glory in his poverty, and in his own nothingness.

"GLADLY will I glory in my infirmities,"† in my poverty, in this, namely, that I am nothing of myself, that

---

* Cant. ii. 12. † II. Cor. xii. 9.

the very power and strength, and true riches of Christ may dwell in me. For I despair of myself altogether, and nought of confidence or strength remaineth in me, and nothing is due to me, save every evil and trouble and distress. Nay, I desire not to be anything at all, that Thou, Thou the Highest Good mayest be all, and that in Thee may be my full glory, but in me nothing. For I. am a poor wandering and lost little sheep, or I am even as "*a dove that is decoyed not having a heart,*"* as a " reed shaken with the wind," as a vineyard that is spoilt, and that bringeth forth thorns and brambles; I am wretched and miserable, and full of darkness and obscurity, subject exceedingly to vanity and changeableness, lightly wavering about from the right hand to the left. And if aught of good or of virtue, or of equity, or of justice, or of truth, or of peace, shall be in me, since Thou Thyself art indeed all goodness itself, and virtue, and equity, and truth, and all the rest, therefore Thou art

---

* Os. vii. 11.

all, and I am wholly nothing. And as the iron which is wholly heated can say: "I indeed burn, but from the fire which is in me, not that I am myself fire;" and as the candle may say: "it is true, I indeed give light, but from the light which is in me, not that I am myself light;" and as every kind of fit instrument may say: "I work indeed, but it is by the hand of the workman;" so the soul is said to burn, not of itself, but from the love that is in it; and it is said to shine, not of itself, but from the light of wisdom and truth that is in it, and it is said to work, but it is God Who worketh all things therein. And if these things shall depart from the soul, that is to say, love, and wisdom, and light, it will remain cold and in darkness. But as an instrument, however fit it may be, lieth wholly useless and fruitless, unless the hand of the workman worketh by means of it; so too the soul, however nobly it may have been created, and however full of genius and intellect, yet lieth empty and fruitless, unless God work thereby all His works.

Chapter XXIII.

Of true self-resignation.

SINCE things happen with such marvellous variety, and divers accidents upon which we could never have presumed, occur so unexpectedly, while those things which had rendered the soul very anxious, oftentimes never come to pass at all, therefore it is that in this wretched life there is nothing better or more full of peace or more pleasing unto our God, than in all things to have no care about one's self, and to despise whatever, either from defect or vice, may be found therein, tending to one's own convenience, and to suffer our Lord, with a free heart, to work out our salvation in His own way, whether this be by means of convenience or inconvenience, by consolation or desolation, by death or by life, by darkness or by light, in whatsoever way that it shall please Him. And thus frequently and utterly resigning himself unto his Lord, whatever may happen to him let a man accept from the Hand of his Lord, as the best thing that can come to him. In this way he will not be anxious about daily events, whether they shall happen in this manner or in that, for in themselves they are neither good nor bad; nor will he feel in the depth of his living being a choice for the one or a distaste for the other, but just as the aforesaid things occur, so do they please him well, so far, that is to say, as they touch his interior being, because he is content with all that God may order. But an inclination to what is desirable in itself, and aversion to what is despicable (with regard, namely, to those things which may be held in common both by the good and the wicked,) let him in no wise follow, save only so far as may serve to his own profit. And so let him become accustomed to found and set himself firmly in the One, Highest, Eternal, and Incommutable Good, which no accidents can reach, and which, when all others shall forsake him, will never leave him, but however desperate may be the things that happen to him, will faithfully remain true to him as his friend. And with this Highest Good he will remain firmly fixed, walking continually with earnestness and sincerity before the Face of God day and night in all truth and wisdom, in which he will be confirmed so as not to be turned away, and which will "*go down with him into the pit, and will not leave him in bands*,"* and will show unto him the pure truth concerning doubtful things; and he shall look therein at all things, in his own measure, even according as the One, Highest, and Incommutable Good in which he is founded, understandeth, and did understand when by His Eternal Wisdom He made all things. And this Wisdom will be a companion to him upon his journey, and at home, and in every place and at all times, a never-failing light in darkness, a pleasant friend to talk with, who

---

* Wisd. x. 13, 14.

will keep him exceeding gladsome company at times of silence and of leisure, an inward unction that lighteneth every trouble. Guarded by the friendship of this companion, he will want no other, but will abound within in all things, because he possesseth that in which all things are. And in his poverty, that is to say, because he is destitute of all worldly comfort and consolation, and because all things are destitute of him, he will be as liberal and bounteous inwardly with that companion of his, as if he were lord of the whole world. He may be clothed in sackcloth, sprinkled over with ashes, deprived of the light of day; he may be the last and most despised of all, he may be hidden in a corner of the house, and be burdened with many inconveniences; or, on the contrary he may be held in honour and respect, all outward things may be just the opposite to those above-mentioned; yet none of these affect him, for whatever he may desire, he clearly possesseth in this Wisdom, of whose fulness neither adversity nor trouble take aught away. This is the straight path of the elect of God, the path of Truth and Wisdom, and they who keep to it under every circumstance come happily to the wished-for end, so that the evil spirit shall be able to find in them little or nothing of his own at the time of their departure from the world.

Chapter XXIV.

How he who is poor in spirit is exceeding rich.

A CERTAIN man being truly poor in spirit and strengthened by our Lord, speaking of the higher part of his soul, thus saith: Behold, I am rich and abound, for I already have all that I desire of this world, and even that which I have, I have it as if I had it not, because it is not with love that I possess it, and I can be without it and yet suffer no harm to myself. The highest, naked, formless and incommutable Truth keepeth itself in the highest part of my spirit, and showeth unto me its ineffable riches, which are beyond all comparison, even the One, Simple Word, in Whom all things are contained, and beyond Whom I require nothing else. In Him is shown unto me my own nothing, and the non-being of myself, inasmuch as I am myself, and all the vices which might incline my mind to one side or another, and also there is shown unto me the *True Being* of all things. Nor do I look from below at the lower kind of accidents and circumstances, according to the changeableness of sensuality, but from above do I look at all things, and the Truth crieth out for me with a terrible voice to all strange things that are not at one with it: " Come not here, for the place where *I* stand is holy ground." And thus very frequently doth the Truth show me His face in the choir, and in my bed, and at table, and in my cell, and in the midst of outward tumult, and labours and various occupations;* and He teacheth

---

* Compare B. Henry Suso, Hor. Æt. Sap. i. 6.

me ever to simplify within me all things that are from without, and to change them into such interior unity as may give fresh strength. And so powerful is His Face, that it mightily subdueth the heart and the body, so that not only the foundations, but *even* the " hinges and lintels"* of the temple of the Lord are moved to correspond and agree with It, and (the whole being) is moved to follow speedily whithersoever He goeth, and to follow up with its whole strength the light shown to it, and to offer without intermission all that it is, and may be, together with everything created in time and in eternity. And then it would be unto me a great consolation and solace of heart, if even in the body I were able to bow myself below all created things, and keep myself there depressed, and humbled, and abject. And almost (so far as relateth to myself and to vices) He bringeth me down to nothing,

---

* The Ed. Prin. has "*subliminaria cordium*," evidently a corrupt reading for "*superliminaria cordium.*" Compare Amos ix. 1.

that is, He showeth how all things that are not united with Him are nothing. And after that I have thus fainted away before His Face, He next taketh my voluntary look, and impresseth it and uniteth it immediately with His own look, so that mine and His form one clear look, and not such a look as is reflected from every side, so that in it, and with it, I look at all things that are or can be, in my measure, even as that Face of His. And thereby I am made careless about myself, and comforted concerning all that may happen unto me. And whatever hath leave to come over me from the incommutable Truth and eternal disposition of my Lord, to Whom I have resigned my life and death, and all that I am and may be in time and in eternity, to that do I also give leave, yet without presuming rashly in aught, or choosing aught for my own convenience.

Chapter XXV.

How blessed a thing it is to rise in soul above every outward exaltation, and to sink below every humiliation.

LET all things be to thee, saith the Truth Itself, even as they are to Me, simple creatures. Whatsoever falleth into the memory concerning all things which the soul of man can desire save only God, even in those things that seem to be holy from without, and which if a man had, he would not on that account be in anything more holy or blessed, nor if he had them not would he be less holy or blessed; all these things move me not to desire them any more than dry wood, or the flower which is trampled underfoot, for all these things have withered in my heart. And on the other hand I can with a free and humble heart undergo what sensuality fleeth from and avoideth where-ever it can, so that on either side all things are broken through by one simple and naked gaze. All men in general do I heartily venerate as the throne of the glory of the Holy Trinity, and each man in particular do I hold to be one who will be infinitely higher than I shall be in future bliss: although indeed as for myself I am not worthy even to be the least, nor to presume any such thing of myself. Thus do I reverence all, but of no one have I any ill-dread, so as to be inwardly oppressed by him, in that perchance he is powerful and hard, or that I shall have to suffer this or that at his hands. For what if I am oppressed, vexed, contemned and despised without any fault of mine; if I am the least of all, and the least esteemed at home, uncared for, cast aside as a vessel unfit for use, all the days of my exile, or whatever sensual affection might dread; shall such things or any like them ever reach unto me, up there on high where I act, or rather am acted on, suffering the divine inaction, in which I desire, and fear nothing strange?

Before the face and in the face of the incommutable Truth, I rise in soul above every outward exaltation, and sink in affection below every humiliation which can be done unto me by men, however much tribulations and inconveniences may abound. You therefore I call blessed, and you glorious, and none others, who are thus lifted up above every appetite, and are thus sunk down in a free heart below every depression, wheresoever or whosoever ye may be, whether of necessity constituted in honour or dignity, or despised and desolate. For in this respect I look neither to the habit, nor the stature, nor the state, nor the degree, nor good health of body, nor outward pomp, nor indeed aught outward whatsoever, however great in appearance, for all these things our Lord doth not greatly regard, nor are they to be held for much. Nor have I any great care in this respect, how it may happen unto me in outward matters, whether, namely, I am clothed in sackcloth or in good clothes, whether I dwell in a corner at home, or otherwise, whether I be despised or had in reverence, whether others be preferred before me or not; for all these things in whatsoever way they may happen, cannot touch me. For small and slight indeed is still the spiritual conversation of a man, and weak and nigh unto destruction the state of his mind, if he be yet agitated by such outward things, or vacillate to and fro between what is to be followed and what is to be avoided. And too exceeding great a disgrace is it in the sight of our Lord, that a soul so noble, and susceptible of the Highest Good in itself, should care about such vile and unworthy things.

Chapter XXVI.

Of the double region, that is, of the lower region of sensuality, and the higher, of the reformed soul.

THE lower region, that is, the region of sensuality, is full of disquiet, disturbance, and conflict. Therefore with one's whole strength ought one to hasten to the higher region and state of soul· And then, when we shall be masters of ourselves in truth, our footsteps will not be straitened, but freely and liberally shall we walk with our Lord, looking at all things with Him. With Him also shall we go forth to all things that are or are done, and there-from shall we return again unto the Self-Same, in all things being at peace and at rest in God, even although the lower region with its many powers shall be agitated by adversity, and by different motions according to the passions and inclinations of each. For however much progress we shall make, nature must ever remain nature; but in nought do these motions of nature belong to the higher state of soul; and if the latter shall prevail, it shall not be subjected to, nor in any way driven by nature. We may indeed have divers consolations, even not of a bad kind, or sensible devotions, so as to rest in them, yet remain imperfect and unstable, and inwardly unfounded in the knowledge and love of truth and justice.

And so all the days of our life we wander about, with the desire indeed of making progress and of more speedily arriving at the perfect state of soul; but yet we see not the inward way by which we must go, by reason of those outward things with which we have been satisfied, and so we make no farther progress. But the path by which we arrive without hindrance at the Highest Good, at our first origin, at the peace of God, is this, namely, that we love the Cross of our Lord, by following His footsteps, lest we place our peace and rest too much in outward things, and insensible devotions; and that we live without choosing our own convenience, and without avoiding what is inconvenient. For as long as we are content with our own rest, and our own convenience, we shall be troubled, and we shall vacillate according to what happeneth to us from without. Therefore continually ought we to recall our mind from what is without to that which is within, and there will be shown unto us the path by which we may arrive at the highest peace. Outward showing profiteth but little, unless by an inwardly keen glance we learn by experience which way to go. And this is why we remain dry and in darkness, without the illumination of truth, because we have not arrived at that which is essential in all things,* because of which all external things are made and are, even those that are mystical and spiritual. However much we seem to have made progress outwardly in spiritual goods and appearances, or in the reputation of sanctity, all is empty and little, unless the interior man be re-formed and con-formed to God. But what if he shall be conformed? Whatsoever God shall refuse to give of other outward things and estimation, gladly will we be without, because it is not necessary for us; for as much as we shall be in our inmost being blessed and holy, so much will all that is outward be sanctified for us by this very reason, and rendered acceptable to our Lord. Outward things of themselves do not sanctify us. And

---

* "quid rei."

although all things ought to be done "decently and in order," yet must we not rest in such things, for often are they an impediment to our true progress, in as much as we abide and rest in them, instead of proceeding through them to true and the highest sanctity. It is impossible that we should be truly and inly spiritual, as long as we are content with outward good and other appearances, in which we delay, and beyond which we do not pass. Of a truth, unless we from the bottom of our hearts deny ourselves, the Spirit of Truth, "Who will teach us all truth,"* and Who will grant unto us inwardly to walk before our Lord, and Who will make all our interior to correspond with Him, will not come unto us. And "*why have we spent our silver for that which is not bread, and our labour for that which does not satisfy us?*"† And why do we not rather buy all fulness, and satiety, and all that is desirable, at a small price? For unless we give what we love and possess, we

---

* John, xvi. 13.   † Isa. lv. 2.

shall not have what we desire. Hence it is that we are cast down by grief, and are straitened in ourselves, and are poured out in useless affection; and hence too come aversions, and hence it comes to pass that what happeneth to us from without, our Lord so disposing, agreeth not with our taste; hence also arise such great instability and interior tumults, even there, where they are unbecoming. Hence, lastly, cares and occupations obtain possession of us, since we have inwardly no power over ourselves, so that they indeed operate, whilst we miserably suffer. All these things come to us, because our conversation is from without, and because from below and not from above we look at what is itself beneath us. Who is he, who is now in darkness, and the light is not in him? Let him come to our Lord, the light that never faileth, and lean inwardly upon Him.* Where is He? he asketh. "The word is nigh thee, even in thy mouth and in thy heart, in thy senses,

---

* Isa. l. 10.

within thee, without thee, above thee, beneath thee, round about thee on every side wheresoever thou shalt come; the Word, namely, simple and only, the Spouse; the Word which frequently is present to minds burning with love, and which often manifesteth unto them all good, wisdom, truth, justice, peace, and light eternal; illuminating all that come to Him. What then remaineth, save to open our eyes, and see and understand the advent of our Lord unto us, and to stand humbly waiting for Him?

God therefore cometh unto us mediately, that is to say, through grace, that is, through wisdom, truth, justice, and the rest. If now we love God and are in grace, "all things work together for us unto good," without acceptation of one or another; yea, even in all those events which seem to have happened for our destruction. Our very passions also and natural inclinations and all things which appear to us impediments, if we be watchful, confer no small advantage upon us. For when the soul is beset by such, straightway they cause her to run back to our Lord, and to her own interior, and to that higher region of hers, where they cannot reach her. And where her own strength and fortitude fail, there she seeketh true fortitude, and is humbled by her own weakness. Our Lord, Who from everlasting hath loved us so exceedingly, and hath shown unto us such great proofs of love, and moreover giveth unto us His whole self, how could He suffer aught to come upon us, save for our advantage and for His love? And if perchance on account of our fault, He suffereth aught so to come, and leaveth us? Well—then we shall feel this, namely, that we have deserved infinitely more, and gladly will we undergo whatsoever shall seem good unto Him. Thus ought we in divers ways to reach unto our Lord, according as different things happen unto us, and in all things to possess grace, and in every tribulation and trouble to say with the Prophet Jeremias: "*Clearly this is mine own evil, and I will bear it.*" He who is diligent in grace, and attendeth thereto, understandeth well how our Lord ordaineth all things for our profit, and will have as much in the least as in the greatest, as much in darkness as in light, and will bring forth darkness into light, and want into abundance. For grace is as it were a ring or a circle, not having beginning nor end; for it operateth and proceedeth forth from God unto all creatures, and from creatures again without intermission it tendeth back to its origin. When therefore with our highest powers we are united with our Lord, we proceed forth to all things together with Him through His grace. For what He permitteth we permit, what He giveth, we give: walking in a certain way outside the sense of the flesh. With Him also we suffer to come upon us whatever shall happen, whether from without or from within, contempt, infirmity, passions, and the rest: as if a man were to say in his necessities: "This hath been so preordained from everlasting, so then ought it to happen, and so I will it to happen, and not otherwise do I choose. Our Lord hath given me infirmities, dryness, passions, and darkness; in these then I wish to exercise myself, just as if in my heart I had strong sensible feeling about God, and from this seek to gather fruit. For out of His great love hath our Lord ordained that these should come upon me for the increase and as an occasion of my profit and eternal salvation. There then shall our light rise in darkness, and our darkness shall be as the noon-day.* There shall we possess God, and God will possess us in that most hidden knowledge, in which all that can happen unto us from without will not be able to reach us. There are we hidden in the secret of the face of our Lord.† Thanks be to God Almighty, that no one seeth us there. Thanks be to God, that nothing appeareth unto the eyes of flesh, save every infirmity, lest the robustness which lieth hidden might be taken away, were it seen. According to this union ought we to look at all things, not according to ourselves, and thus strive ever

---

* Is. lviii. 10.   † Ps. xxx. 21.

more and more to come out of ourselves. Nor let any one think us straitened, or in want, or wretched, or without glory, because peradventure all external comfort is withdrawn from us; that is to say, because no man seeketh us, or asketh after us, or because we are cast out, oppressed, thought of no renown; or because we have such a contempt for ourselves, as to choose rather to be poor, and in a certain sense to be esteemed as the offscouring of all. As our Lord liveth, in Whose sight we walk in sincerity and truth, according to this way of looking at things there is nothing necessary for us of all those other things that are wanting to us; for nothing else do we require save that Highest Good, in which we have all things. All other things besides that are to us exceeding small and little, and if He give them not, gladly will we be without them, treating them as superfluities. But if nature is disturbed, burdened, and undergoeth with but little pleasure inconveniences and contradictions, and is disquieted because she hath not her own will, that is nothing to us: only let her remain in the lower place, lest likewise she involve the soul. But for this very reason, the unction which cometh down from above, and falleth down *upon the beard*, that is to say, upon the higher powers of the soul, at times also falleth down upon the *skirt of the garment*,* namely, in cordial feeling, and on all the senses of the flesh; so that even these for the time desire nothing else, than that the will of our Lord should be done on this earth of ours, as it is in heaven. In this way their murmuring and impatience cease, and they bear more lightly inconveniences and tribulations. And if thus we follow up the grace of God, not turning away outside it, then too we shall be ever in the light; if not indeed in the light and taste of the senses and affections, at least in that light, than which we require and desire no other, save what our Lord shall be pleased to give, be it darkness or light.

---

* Ps. cxxxii. 2.

Chapter XXVII.

How strictly God will require the reformation or the amelioration as well of our interior as of our exterior.

WITHOUT ceasing will I strive to be inwardly renewed before the Face of our Lord, Who looketh at all my interior and the very bottom of my intention in the light of His own most just and irreversible judgment, even in everything that moveth or attracteth me, so as to see whether I hold aught of value, which is of no value to Him. And He strictly requireth the conformity of my whole interior with His own image, and of my exterior with His own conversation in the flesh: so that not a part only, but the whole of my undivided self, He claims for Himself; since He it is Who hath wholly made me, and wholly redeemed me, and

Who willeth not that the throne of His glory for any cause whatsoever should be disturbed or disquieted, judging that nothing in the whole world could be worthy or powerful enough to oppress or corrupt the temple of His truth. And it is His will too that we give ourselves up to Him, and keep solemn festival with Him, exercising a great authority over ourselves, and over everything else which might disturb us. And it is His desire that we be joined with Him and enjoy Him, as if constituted wholly outside ourselves; making but little account of, despising, and utterly annihilating ourselves, caring nothing whatever for what may happen unto us either from without or from within, so that all our liberty and security may come from no other source than profound humility, self-denial, and conformity with the eternal and incommutable truth and wisdom, which should wholly possess all our outward and inward powers, operating by them, as by voluntary and living instruments. So also it is His will, that beyond and through all things we should look at the face of wisdom, truth, justice, and the peace of God, that is to say, according to the measure of our littleness, and in order to free ourselves from all things, however turbulently they may happen. For however much tribulations and obstacles may abound, yet there ever remaineth a glorious path, exceeding wide and straight, which passeth through the midst of all tribulations. Therein are we taught, not by turning aside or by flying away, but by a mature, spiritual, and strengthened gaze, abiding at rest in all things with the very incommutable truth, to rise above all impediments. We are taught also to regard with gentleness all the marvelling, seriousness, empty displeasure of every one else, and if we are not able to correct the ill-will of others with equanimity, at least to suffer it, as though standing in safety, and placed under secret guardianship, where none of these things can reach us.

Chapter XXVIII.

Exhortation to conform ourselves to the image of God.

WHO can worthily weigh in his mind how without intermission our Lord looketh at and considereth His own eternal image in us, which can never be blotted out: how He seeth and knoweth Himself in us, as though (so far as may be) capable of being received whole and undivided by us? For He enjoyeth Himself in us, and we enjoy Him in Himself, and in ourselves. Strictly also doth He require conformity to that image after which we have been created, being Himself vehemently zealous on our behalf. Shall not the Lord of glory show zeal for the temple and throne of His glory? For this reason He at times taketh all our powers, not only the higher, but also sometimes the lower, and uniteth them with Himself, causing them to be powerless to operate, so that there may be no contradiction, but that He Himself may possess us wholly, and that we, giving ourselves up to Him,* may suffer His operation. Blessed is he who thus in himself suffereth the operation of God. Who will give unto me often to undergo this blessed passion, whereby I may forget myself and all things, and nothing may enter into me with relish, save the Word Bridegroom, Who then inwardly and outwardly possesseth my whole being?

---

* The Ed. Prin. here reads: "*nos ipsum, vacantes, ejus.*" Strange's reading is followed in the text. Whichever reading be adopted, it is clear that our own will is not excluded from co-operation with God.—*Trans.*

Chapter XXIX.

The heritage of the poor in spirit in this life.

MY inheritance in this life is not, nor shall be, any other, nor will I esteem aught else, than to be hidden, and abject, and the last of all, so that no man may seek after me, nor enquire for me, nor care for me; just as if I were of no moment, no estimation, poor and despicable. Therefore, with my whole strength, day and night, inwardly and outwardly, I will watchfully aim at wishing for these and the like things, so that when they come I may receive them as gifts which I had lately, and also for long desired. Great things then I leave to the great, the learned, and the famous; with none of these have I to do; but gladly will I be content with little and with the least, as though I were of no value. For me the Face alone of the Bridegroom is enough.

Chapter XXX.

Of the praise of holy poverty, and how by voluntary bearing of adversity we arrive at the clarification of the soul.

O HOW glorious is the poverty of our Lord Jesu, and of all His elect. With what praises to extol Thee I know not, for all riches, glory, honour, praise and abundance are in Thee. For if we are spiritual, interior, subtle, and ingenious; if we are clever, and know how to bring forth deep things out of heavenly and hidden mysteries, but are not drawn to the poverty and simplicity of our Lord Jesu, little or nothing will be our edification; for what is interior is not seen, and doth not edify. To be drawn to poverty therefore is to show forth humility, simplicity, and abjection, in all things and through all things, where the cause demandeth it, always to choose what is simpler, viler, and lowest; hardly to take what is necessary of temporal things; to embrace the cross, and grievances, and labours, and what others abhor, and so to converse, as if all our motions, behaviour and works should cry out, 'our kingdom is not of this world.' These are the things, and others like to them, which sanctify us, edify those who are looking on, and which have ever preserved religion stable, and still preserve it. For our Lord Jesus hath left us His cross to carry, and not soft things nor sweet, nor conveniences; not the vain praise of men, but every kind of tribulation, sufferings, inconveniences; miseries, and aversion to sensuality, so that we may be as those who have nothing in common with the world, as long as we live. O how sweet is the yoke of Christ! Thou who freely in thy heart hast subjected thyself to this yoke, behold, all things are light to thee. For on this account disturbances, grievances, and aridities are in us, and come to us, namely, because we seek to fly from and avoid the cross and the yoke, nor do we submit ourselves with love. When therefore the cross and yoke of our Lord have for us a relish, and we are drawn to them, and when also we are refreshed by humiliations, and littleness, and poverty, then in a short time shall we pass through all impediments, and then shall we account reproach for joy, and humiliation for exaltation, and want for abundance. Then shall we as it were *die daily, and behold we shall live ;** we shall be abject and without glory, and yet full of glory ; we shall be counted as nothing and the reproach of men of no moment and estimation, and behold we shall be as *those of whom the world is not worthy :*† we shall be desperate and without hope, and behold our hope will be exceeding great, and our security interior, in which no one will see us from without, nor reach to us, and in which we shall dwell with our Lord, fortified on every side with the shield of truth and of equity, and yet not in vain bound or hemmed in; otherwise we should have

---

* II. Cor. vi. 9.   † Heb. xi. 37, 38.

to blush greatly when we shall stand before our Lord both now and afterwards. Now, being such, we know and have known no man,* or no thing according to affection, or the inclinations of sensuality: for looking at heaven and earth, and all that in them is, or hath been made, never are we corrupted by the love of anything, nor are we straitened by fear, and this, because the Word of God Himself, the highest, eternal, and incommutable truth, wisdom, and justice, holding rule over our mind, driveth away the darkness, illuminateth the intellect, and so uniteth it, that in its simple gaze there is no retrogression, nor reflection; moreover, in the conjunction and embrace of our face and His, (according to a certain measure,) there is nothing which cometh between. And in this conjunction, through Him we see all things and Himself; and therein too He enjoyeth and seeth Himself through us, where He is Himself the very sight,

---

* II. Cor. v. 16. "Wherefore henceforth we know no man according to the flesh."

both He Who is seen, and He Who seeth. And so it cometh to pass that our illuminated intellect, seeing all things in wisdom and in truth, by no means suffereth for the time our memory or simple introverted thought to be in any wise obscured by any objects; consequently neither the will nor the affection doth it suffer to be in any wise disquieted by strange desires. Where then we thus present to our Lord His own pure and undepicted image, there are we released from labour, and nothing remaineth to us of our own. And there He maketh us love out of love, and truth out of truth, and wisdom out of wisdom, and all good out of Himself. There are we born sons by adoption, taken up in the Only Begotten Son by the Father, to Whom inwardly and outwardly, according to the measure of our littleness we are made conformable.

Chapter XXXI.

In what way the interior man is clarified, and united with the Word, and that in whatever happeneth, and in all we do, we have need of a simple eye and a pure intention.

LET Him kiss me with the kiss of His mouth,* saith the soul wounded with love. Truly a great desire, and beyond the measure of a man's own poor experience. But because *love taketh no comfort in what is impossible*,† or in weak things that perish, therefore whatever may be heaped upon us besides this, is to us exceeding small and little, neither quieting nor satisfying our desire. When, therefore, the Eternal Wisdom or Uncommutable Truth showeth us His Face, His incomparable

---

* Cant. i. 1.   † Chrysolog. Serm. 147.

riches, all beauty, and all that is desirable, and how he who beholdeth His Face desireth nothing further; then our interior face striveth with such vehement love to be pressed against His Face in an interior kiss and embrace, chaste and powerful, as if wholly it ought to pass into it and be transformed, and in a certain manner itse'f become what that Face of His is in itself. Therein the Eternal Father generateth without intermission His only simple Word, in Whom we know and see all things, and by Whom we learn ever to simplify and unify our multiplicities, and occupations, and our outward actions, by looking at Him beyond and through all our works, however great and divine they may appear, and in Whom alone we shall rest and be made stable, and by a mutual regard our gaze shall be made one with His and indifferent. Therein eye is against eye, face against face: there is the face of the Bridegroom, and there is our face, yet the dissimilitude is not small, about which however we say nothing for the present. Therein our created life without intermission looketh at and visiteth our uncreated life, which is from everlasting in God, and one thing with Him. Hence we are made as humble and little in ourselves before the Face of our Lord, as a child one moment old, nor can we annililate ourselves enough according to our desire. This making little and annihilation of ourselves causeth us to be as liberal, free, secure, and abounding, as if we had need of none other. From this we have a simple eye and intention in all our thoughts, motions, and works, and this simple eye* so seriously and cautiously looketh at every object, as if to say to each: " I see what thou art, what is in thee, what thou intendest, whence thou comest, and whither thou goest, and thou hast a relish for me

---

* The simple eye is not the same thing as the pure intention, as a little further on the holy writer carefully distinguishes between them. It is not clear from the original, whether in this passage, it is the simple eye or the intention which scrutinizes every object, but as it is afterwards said that it is the former which performs this office, while the pure intention follows after it to penetrate deeper into the truth, I have referred it to the former.—*Trans.*

just in proportion with what thou art, and not otherwise." On this account liberal and speedy is our progress in following after our Lord, after wisdom and truth, after the Bridegroom, *whithersoever He goeth*,* according to the measure of our littleness, since from no other source are we helplessly weakened, nor do we know anything in this respect, either in heaven above, or on the earth below, for in Him whatsoever agitateth us, disquieteth and blindeth our interior eye, although it may seem outwardly a holy affection, yet in Him is altogether hurtful and unworthy, dividing us from true union with the Highest Good, and generating a hindrance and a veil between God and our illuminated reason. Therefore will it stand in need of the burning and purgation of fire in us; therefore in all that happeneth unto us inwardly or outwardly, above all things there are necessary for us a simple eye and a pure intention: a simple eye to examine maturely what each thing is

---

* Apoc. xiv. 4.

[...] His [...] permission looketh
[...] reason nor [...] life, which
[...] everlasting in God, and one thing
with Him. Hence we are made as humble and little in ourselves before the Face
of our Lord as a child one moment old,
nor can we annihilate ourselves enough
according to our desire. This making
little and annihilation of ourselves causeth
us to be as [...] free, secure, and
abounding as if we had need of none
other. From this we have a simple eye
and intention in all our thoughts, motions,
and works, and this simple eye* so
seriously and curiously looketh at every
object, as if to say to each: "I see what
thou art, what is in thee, what thou intendest, whence thou comest, and whither
thou goest, and thou hast a relish for me

---

* The simple eye is not the same thing as the pure intention,
as a little further on the [...] which [...] y distinguishes
between them. It is not clear [...] the original, whether in
this passage it is the simple eye or the [...] which
looks at every object, but as it is after[...] the
former which performs this office, w[...]
[...] penetrate deeper into th[...]
former.—*Trans.*

hout
For
and
the
tims
And
orld
eth
care
our-
for
of
and
not
in?
d of
the
l evil
united
equity,
as on a
y impedi-
being made
ssipateth and

according to the right truth, which discerneth the precious from the vile; a pure intention, to follow after the simple eye, and to see the truth in all things, and this causeth us to be wholly empty of everything belonging to self, and to be comforted in everything that can come upon us. It causeth us to perform, with a free and unchained heart, without expectation or hesitation, all that is truly virtuous before our Lord and men, and in like manner all that we do inwardly and outwardly, without any other regard, or for the sake of anything. By this we are freed from all vain scrupulosity and anxiety, from the fear of hell and of the devil, from dread of divers accidents, and of perverse men, and of divers feelings, however great they may outwardly be; in a word, from everything that can straiten us. By this are we led on by the broad paths of justice and equity,* and in security we say: 'Even though I should walk in the midst of the shadow of death, I will fear no evils."† By this we have confi-

---

* Prov. iv. 11.   † Ps. xxii. 4.

dent access to our Lord, and without shame we stand before His face. For hence is it, that our words are great and urgent, and our colloquy pleasant with the King, the Lord of Hosts, devoted victims though we be, and a holy oblation. And from all these things the whole world becometh vile to us, and all that belongeth thereto. For this reason we take no care to consider or superfluously occupy ourselves with the things of the world, for why should we turn aside from the face of wisdom and be turned to foolishness and lies, such as is everything which is not truth and wisdom, or is not therein? Then also is fulfilled therein that word of Solomon: "*The king that sitteth on the throne of judgment, scattereth away all evil with His look.*"* For the soul united with the simple truth, wisdom and equity, which reside in its higher part as on a throne of judgment over every impediment and creature-ship, and being made one simple look therewith, dissipateth and

---

* Prov. xx. 8.

bringeth to nought by its own strengthened look every evil, every dissimilitude, every veil and obstacle between itself and our Lord ; or rather, all these things are dissipated by the look of God, by Himself as the severe and just judge of all things that can molest and disquiet us, and Who placeth a boundary to them which they shall not pass, saying: "Hitherto shalt thou come and shalt go no further."* Thus then every obstacle being scattered and broken, the voice of the chaste turtle which yet liveth in the land of the sorrowing is frequently heard in the land of the living; for all motions of one who orderly converseth before the face of our Lord, his behaviour and thought, his inward and outward conversation, are (as it were) powerful voices before our Lord. Nay, even when he sleepeth, his innocence, purity, equity, modesty, and other proofs of love cease not to utter their cries in the ears of the Bridegroom. *Many daughters have gathered together riches,* honours,

---

* Job xxxviii. 11.

glory, consolations, and the rest, *but this one hath surpassed them all*,* counting all other things for little, and despising them. The mere face and kiss of the Bridegroom suffice for her, in Whom she hath all things, and requireth nothing farther. If none of those outward things which are desired and sought after by others, be given her, not less will be her glory and fulness; if all things be added unto her, they will be none the greater. Therefore can she do without all things and suffer no loss. Let others then seek whatever they will, one this thing and another that; let them covet, and acquire, be agitated and moved, and inwardly taken up with all sorts of strange desires: these she accounts not for great, finds nothing precious in them, nothing glorious, nothing pleasant save the face of her Lord and the kiss of her spouse; all the rest is vile to her and withered. For she is one of the chaste virgins and pure brides of the Bridegroom, who, uncorrupted by any

---

* Prov. xxxi. 29.

existing thing, nor helplessly weakened or held back, followeth the Bridegroom, according to her poor little measure, whithersoever He goeth. For she hath a true knowledge of all existing things, as they exist, and a simple knowledge of the truth, nor doth she look on the face of any thing, in so far as it moveth, otherwise than the truth judgeth it ought to be moved. And well is she ordered on the right hand and on the left, in all that happeneth, so that to her the Bridegroom is both life and to live, and her interior man is made like unto Him by Whom, and according to Whose image it hath been made. All her outward conversation also is, so to speak, formed by interior virtues; an image, as it were, of a perfect soul, and reformed, as becometh a chaste spouse: so that there is nothing in her interior man to spot and corrupt her true virginity and integrity, nothing outward in words, or look, or behaviour, shameless or impure, nothing, in a word, unbecoming in any of her motions. Otherwise in no wise could she be called chaste, but an adulteress, if she were held back by anything whatsoever, unless she were quickly to repent, if also she were inwardly to frame strange images, with which she might commit adultery, and be turned away from God. And how greatly these abound in the soul no man knoweth, save he who for the most part hath been already freed therefrom. But because lower down, in her lower part, she is on every side agitated and blown about, she must needs raise herself up at times out of the noise, and the multiplicity of all the things with which she might have to do battle, and place herself there, where not only she seeth nothing to desire, nothing to amuse her, or weary her, but where all her powers are vividly intent upon the one highest good, that is to say, the Bridegroom. And here she findeth neither time, nor place, nor state, nor habit, nor any kind of conflict, for here these things are not necessary, but a certain pure existence, into which no accidents can come. There she seeth all good, and the breadth of charity and truth, and the fairness of jus-

―――――――――――――――――――

―――― ――― ―― ――――― ――――― ―
―― ――― ――――― ―― Bridegroom
―――――― ― ―― ――― little measure
――――― ―― ―― ――. For she hath a
―― ―――――― ―― all existing things, as
――― ―――, and a simple knowledge of the
――― ―― ――― she look on the face of any
――― ― ―― ―― as ― moveth, otherwise than
―― ――― ――――― ― might it be moved.
And well is she moved in the right hand
and in the left in all that happeneth, so
that in her the Bridegroom is both life
and in life, and her interior man is made
like unto Him by Whom, and according
to Whose image it hath been made.
All her outward conversation also is, so
to speak, formed by interior virtues; an
image, as it were, of a perfect soul, and reformed, as becometh a chaste spouse: so
that there is nothing in her interior man
to spot and corrupt her true virginity and
integrity, nothing outward in words, or
look, or behaviour, shameless or impure,
nothing, in a word, unbecoming in any of
her motions. Otherwise in ――― ― could
she be called chaste, b―― ――― ―ress, if

The Fiery Soliloquy with God

she were held back by anything whatsoever, unless she were quickly to repent
if also she were inwardly to frame some
images, with which she might commit
adultery, and be turned away from it.
And how greatly these abound in some,
no man knoweth, save he who for the
most part hath been already withdrawn
from. But because he cannot be in the
lower part, she is so tossed and troubled
and blown about, she cannot recollect
herself up at times, and this because of
the multiplicity of the objects, upon
which she might have settled, or might
place herself thereupon, whereas she
seeth nothing to content or satisfy
her, or weary her thereof, but that there
are vividly in her some images of the
good, that is truly and simply so.
And here she findeth the resting
place, nor need she fear any further
conflict, for there is no more trouble
necessary, it being the only centre
into which she can recover herself, and
she seeth in purity, in simplicity, in charity as they are.

tice, and the most straight line of equity, to which she frequently applieth, and with which she compareth all her interior and exterior, the root or deep foundation of her intention, and findeth out what is like or unlike. There she heareth our Lord Himself saying unto her, that all the things which she seeth and feeleth, and which she partly enjoyeth, are all her own, and that eternally she will enjoy them, being transformed into them, if she remain faithful to Him and chaste: namely, that by His grace she may be good in herself, goodness in Him; true, peaceful, wise, virtuous, just, and blessed in herself, truth, peace, wisdom, virtue, equity, blessedness in Him, for by Divine participation we are as gods.* A soul of this sort, abounding in so many lilies, not undeservedly inviteth the Bridegroom to come into her *garden of nuts, to see the fruits of the valleys, and to look if the vineyard hath flourished;* and to *come also into the orchard and the bed of flowers,* to her clean

---

* Ps. lxxxi. 6.

heart, to her ornamented couch, *to the bed of aromatical spices, to feed in the gardens, and to gather lilies*,* where the Spouse is Himself her lilies, her flowers, her cleanness, her ornaments, and her spices. He it is Who feedeth, He it is Who is fed, nor when it is said that the aforesaid are in the bride, or that she hath a clean heart, is anything else meant, than that now in great part she enjoyeth the Spouse. But these things are often repeated, that He Who already is partly present, may come more fully, may bless more richly, and may more frequently show His face, which at times, that He may be more ardently sought for, He hideth; and that what is done as yet in vicissitude and in part, may at last be perfected according to desire in open face.

Truly that is nothing in which hitherto thou hast laboured; thou must apply a wholly different remedy for the sake of interior conformity, rectitude, and equality.

---

* Cant. i. 15; vi. 1, 10.

Otherwise thou wilt fall back into the depth of darkness, dissimilitude and vacillation.

Chapter XXXII.

That virtue in itself standeth unchangeable, nor doth it lie under the power of any accidents.

LET every circumstance or event find thee standing firm like a square stone. Virtue in itself, which is God, abideth ever the same, full and incommutable, nor is it increased or lessened. But the virtue which we have can always decrease and increase as long as we live here. And so much the more precious and more glorious is it in us before our Lord, as agitated by contrary and divers storms, occupations, tumults, and conflicts, it shall be found more constant; nor has it ever truly taken root in us, in time of rest and tranquillity, if it shall fail in time of tribulation. Incomparably sweeter is the virtue which is retained in unfavourable and diverse occasions, than in prosperity and in peace. Virtue in itself is never subjected to, neither is it moved by circumstances. And if it shall unite the soul of man to itself, and make it to be in a certain manner all that it is in itself, namely, by making it a partaker of itself: then, not only doth the soul perform manfully all good, but bravely and with a gentle spirit doth it undergo all that is contrary, as whenever, although it doeth all things well, it is nevertheless reproved, despised, and rejected by others, as of no moment. It knoweth how to see, hear, weigh and consider all things, like and unlike, disturbance and rest, opposition and multiplicity, everything in a word which is and hath been made below God, and yet remain stable and constant, nor be easily impeded by any one, looking at all things with a keen and equal mind, not finding it necessary to avoid, or not to notice one thing or another, however distorted and intricate the circumstances may be. But it forceth everything that moveth it otherwise than it ought, there where it ariseth, to perish and vanish away. For to him who bravely conquereth, and not to him who avoideth the fight, or dissembleth, will be given the hidden manna, and a new name, which no man knoweth save he who receiveth it.* Whatever is thus done in the soul will be firm and solid, so that no matter by what circumstances it may be driven about, it may be likened to a square stone, for it will always safely fall into its own square. If thus it shall be perfect in itself, it will be hurt by nothing strange, but will gain profit in all things. But because it receiveth no consolation out of God, will it then remain without glory and without consolation? Is it a small glory that it hath the knowledge of truth and love, and is able to follow it up; or what is more, that in a certain way it hath been made Love itself by participation? Is it a small glory that it hath acquired conformity both of the inner and outer man;

---

* Apoc. ii. 17.

that it is above all things that are in the world, outside God; that it is hindered by the love of no existing thing, and by the fear of none: in a word, that it so loveth the Lord its God, that forgetful of itself, if it were possible for it to be God, it would wish to be God, so vehemently inflamed is it with love and favour towards Its Lord? There is still another thing, in which when it glorieth, it is most free, namely, in its poverty, littleness, and abjection, that it is cared for by no one in affliction, contempt, and punishment, and that it desireth to be held less and lower than all. By whatever wind it may be driven, it will not be liable to collision, for nothing new or unexpected will happen to it, but all things have been foreseen, and what from everlasting hath been preordained for it, that it waiteth for with evenness of mind. For the Eternal Wisdom, which is more powerful, richer, sweeter, and more glorious than all, goeth ever before it, showing unto it a most fair and broad way. It goeth along with it, leading and confirming it honourably on the way, and it followeth upon its journey, fortifying it on every side in itself, and bringeth it happily to the end. By means of this wisdom it taketh captive in itself every thought and understanding and affection unlike itself. By means of this wisdom it placeth everything that happeneth where it will, and where it ought. To this it directs every conflict and obstacle, so that if possible they may meet with it and fight. Through this wisdom it frequently collecteth all its powers, affections, interior and exterior senses, representing them whole and entire, not held captive in any way by any other power, before the face of the incommutable God, beyond time and place and every accident, and there it placeth itself and all things, where the Eternal Truth placeth them. Nor can the whole world together exalt it as much, or make as much of it and honour it, as it can itself alone despise, contemn, and annihilate itself. On the other hand, looking at it in another light, in respect to abjection, pusillanimity, and scrupulous doubt of its own self, they cannot plunge it in as great dejection, as it alone, with a good conscience for its companion can raise itself up, and abide unshaken on all sides. For the presence of the incommutable truth and equity of God suffereth it not to relish any existing thing, otherwise than He, always powerfully present, judgeth that it ought to be relished. Of all things except God which can be desired by others, whether honour, exaltation, high state, or anything else whatsoever, not so much as can be closed in the eye or contained on the point of a needle, doth it desire; for frequently and most ardently doth it pant after, and place itself above conveniences and inconveniences, sweet and bitter, above and beyond all accidents; and all these things being equally balanced in its mind, one doth not outweigh the others; and also in whatsoever way it shall happen, it desireth nothing further, nor panteth after anything for its own convenience. But all these must remain without, and so to speak, stand dry and useless outside the door, not being able by reason of their imbecility to rush into that state, where the soul, above itself, and all things, enjoyeth the union of the Word. So little care hath he about himself, who is inwardly united with God, that were it for the greater honour of God that he should immediately fall into the depth of hell, rather than be in the highest choir of Angels, he would feel no inward contradiction whatsoever.* And what anxiety can he have about little and daily circumstances, who thus relieved from care about things eternal, liveth free in heart?

Chapter XXXIII.

That besides God nothing can truly comfort the soul.

"LET Him kiss me with the kiss of His mouth." Let the Word, the Bridegroom, unite me to Himself, let Wisdom without intermission generate

---

* See note to chapter xvi.

itself in me, and then to me is it of the very least consequence, if heaven and earth and all that in them is, despise me, for then neither can I be oppressed by these. But if He cast me away from His kiss, then not all the things that exist below God will be able to console me, for what can all the strange things that happen in the world profit a man? To whatever state a man may come, what doth it profit him if he is not united more and more to our Lord, by true internal liberty and purity, being subject to the pressure of nothing earthly, so that to the eyes of the heart all his interior is as plainly clear, as are external things to the eyes of flesh. If he is not drawn more to poverty, abjection, littleness, so that the whole world seemeth a burden to him, and groweth vile; if his behaviour is not more exemplary, mature, and grave, he suffereth no small loss, nor do I care a straw, so to speak, for all the other things to which he may come. But if he shall not perceive his loss, *strangers devour his strength, and he knoweth it not.** Behold he dieth, and in an instant is he called by our Lord,—what shall all things profit him, save only a true union in spirit and conformity with Jesus? That then we may be resolutely renewed wherever we may be, in whatsoever state, place and manner, and under whatsoever circumstances, the Countenance of the Word appeareth unto our countenance; and is so greedy of our poor souls, and strong, that it consumeth and bringeth to nought in us all selfishness, and whatever else is in us save the Word Himself. And He maketh us so poor and little that we are not able sufficiently to bow ourselves down and humble ourselves under every creature, according to our desire. Moreover, He maketh to cease and to keep still every other operation by the presence of His countenance. Hence He earnestly requireth our countenance equally to correspond and to harmonize and be united with Him, and to become partaker of

---

* Osee vii. 9.

Himself. As often therefore as the Eternal Father speaketh, or begetteth effectively and sensibly His own Word in us, then must the soul and all other things be silent, and rest from their operation, and remain there where they are and ought to be. But if it is asked what such a man doth in different events and circumstances, whether for or against, and whether between these things his mind vacillateth? We say, no; because the light of wisdom accompanying him, he can promptly place everything on one side, good or good, wheresoever he will.

CHAPTER XXXIV.

That by the strength of the soul the weakness of nature must be sustained.

WHEN the senate, together with Cæsar, hath been conquered, the free soul exulteth in the fire, and danceth for joy in a virgin body and heart. For when the darkness of the heart hath been dispersed, and when the thongs that have bound it down and burdened it have been loosened, the soul danceth for joy and exulteth in the light of the incommutable Truth, even in the midst of opprobrium, and confusion, and contempt, and torment, and pain, and affliction, both keeping up the feebleness and frailty of nature by the strength of the spirit, and transfusing every accident into the state of its own tranquillity. Lastly, the very changes of things it forceth to contribute to the exercise of its own progress. Never doth it rest in anything that happeneth, even when good, for wherever it hath begun to rest, there its latitude beginneth to fail; but it tendeth ever further and further, and breaketh through all multiplicity, that in any way might hinder the spirit: having ever at hand a whole and perfect introversion to the one highest and incommutable Good, which is ever and everywhere present. And as often as it shall do this, it will find the face, it will find the most chaste, and most sweet kiss of the Bridegroom, and the fruition of the simple

Word of the Father, Which then newly and effectively is generated therein. There will it find infinite latitude, ever in harmony with eternity, or with that which is itself the same as eternity. There is the fulness of all that is desirable, even if the soul be outwardly in great straits. This is of two kinds: first, that it hath all things in common with our Lord, and heareth this voice in the spirit and in the affection: "*My son, all that I have is thine,** and thine is mine;" secondly, that when it feeleth not this, it glorieth eagerly in its own littleness, in its own nothing, in infirmities of heart and body, in divers contrary events and tribulations; it glorieth that it is nothing, nor can do any good of itself; in a word it glorieth in all things that Eternal Providence permitteth to come upon it. Thus God is satisfied with the soul, not only when it acteth virtuously in all prosperity, but also when it beareth every kind of adversity, contempt, and opprobrium with constancy and with a humble

---

* Luke xv. 31.

yet strong heart. Wherefore being united with the Word, the Bridegroom, and being made one thing or one spirit with Him, it saith: "*Often have they fought against me from my youth,** even to this hour, *but they have not prevailed against me.*" Upon my back have they hammered out and forged many tribulations and troubles, and still they do so. But my back, on which wisdom and humility dwell, is so broad, and solid, and strong, that whatever they may choose to forge, cannot burden me so as to make me succumb, for love beareth every burden inwardly and outwardly. *One thing have I desired of the Lord,*† and this is none other than Himself. This, passing by everything else, with my whole strength, day and night, unweariedly will I seek after without intermission. And then farewell all things else, that disagree with that one thing.

---

* Ps. cxxviii. 2, 3. † Ps. xxvi. 1.

Chapter XXXV.

That contemplation is never joined with commotion and disturbance.

WHENEVER a man is beset, disquieted, or taken up with external things which are done by others, then (so to speak) he is out of doors, not within; below, not above. For extraversion into sensual conversation and considerations is an impediment to interior fruition. Never therefore is contemplation joined with commotion; never with troubles, grievances, disturbances, the discussion of other things, scrupulosity, disquietude, from whatever source they may arise. While these last, the union of the Word is never added, that is to say, the most chaste and intransformable embrace of the Bridegroom. But if any man love the Word, the Bridegroom, truly and effectively, so naked, free, strong, and unincumbered by all things must he be, as hardly to have any choice in the least or in the greatest; and just as Eternal Providence shall dispose, so to be wholly content with God, nor to allow his peace of heart to depend in anything on the estimation of men, or on accidents. But however things may happen, let him try beyond and through all things to be ceaselessly renewed by the powerful look and union of the Word: and in this let him maturely and with constancy, inwardly and outwardly, persevere through all things. For this it is necessary for him to prepare a broad, free, unencumbered soul, yes, a soul in no wise straitened, and to exclude everything strange, so that it may not reach the interior of the heart. And he ought in a certain manner to grow hard like flint, in the various things that happen unto him, so that they may hurt him in nothing, but frequently and powerfully be beaten back and recoil. For how can that hurt him which is a gain to him in all things that happen? Of all things therefore that come upon him, or meet him, let him ever think: Our Lord hath sent this or that, in order that I may be more perfect and acceptable to Him.

Chapter XXXVI.

That our Lord Jesus is to be looked at in a twofold way, and of the efflux of love.

IF anything even the least shall begin to burden the heart, let the interior man straightway apply it to the Face of the Word; and it will vanish away. And so in one brief moment let him acquire the custom of unencumbering and emptying himself of many things; of setting many things that are distorted and implicated, each in its own place. And thus there will be no inordinate looking at anything besides God, but with a mature, erect, and firm mind adhering to God, will he dwell and walk in the interior of Jesu our love. There is the infinite breadth, length, height, and depth of all that is desirable. There our Spouse Jesus teacheth us to converse in spirit and in truth without intermission, and admonisheth us to look up and see how His eternal essence, power, and majesty are all one with the Father, and that He is the *brightness of the Father's glory, and the figure of His substance, upholding all things by the word of His power*,* God in the beginning with God, by Whom also all things are made, and out of Whom there is nothing to be desired. He admonisheth us also to look below at His glorious Humanity, full of grace and truth, of all benediction and glory, the Head of all His elect members, our daily refection and nourishment, so that we may drink in spirit and in truth, in interior fatness, His living Blood, which so abundantly floweth without ceasing from His open side, and from which also all good things flow in upon us, and that we may be in a certain measure all that He is Himself. By this we shall be

---

* Heb. i. 3.

made so much to abound, and to be over full, that we shall have continually together with Jesus to flow out upon all creation, that God may be all in all. And this we shall desire to see perfected in every one else, no less than in ourselves, because we ought to desire and wish the favour of all good to all, as cordially as God Himself. And thus we make all the private good of others our own, which is a ready and easy thing to do for those that love, because wherever there is true love there it cannot help flowing out and loving; for there is nought so conformable, nothing so peculiar to deiformity, as continually to flow out, and communicate one's self to others. So also there is no more evident mark and sign of union with the Word than thus without any narrowness to converse in interior breadth of spirit in common love, giving all things, filling all things with Jesu, so that nothing may remain that doth not obtain its right. Thus as far as in us lieth, we are able to fill the heaven and the earth, and all that in them is, with our Love, Who is God.

In the interior therefore of Jesus, we shall have assembled together with Him all the elect, representing them and offering them in breadth and wholeness of heart before the face of the Father as His elect family, laying before Him the miseries and tribulations of all in general, and of some according to the time in particular. Then with our whole heart we offer Him in every place, in spirit, with as great desire as that with which He offered Himself unto the Father. And there between the Godhead and the Humanity, bowing down our spirit in the interior of Jesus, we find peace upon peace, and that chaste love by which we draw all within ourselves and Jesus, and embrace them in simple truth. And united with Him we conquer with ease, by which means we remain whole and unshaken by the various things that happen unto us, because there we lay aside* all impediments, and all that is not the same that is going on in the interior

---

* Strange suggests that we should read "ablegamus" instead of "applicamus."

of Jesu, in broadest effluence. And by bearing with evenness of mind all impediments and oppositions, the whole is reduced to nothing, even as smoke, by this powerful interior look. Therein are we moved to show favour to our enemies, and to those who detract and trouble us, in the same way as to our friends, rulers, and to those who dwell with us, ever yielding gently to the motions of others, and to the wrongs which they do us.

Chapter XXXVII.

That reproof is to be borne with evenness of mind, whether it be just or unjust.

IF the reproof be just it is well, because that taketh place which we desire, and being in harmony with it we add more to it and augment it. If however it be unjust, as for instance about that of which our heart is not conscious, it is nothing to us, because it is only outside us. Nevertheless in all things contrary that can happen, justly or unjustly, in the sight of all or privately, let no murmur be heard either of heart or mouth, no complaint, no superfluous interior involvement, no shakings of the soul, in a word, no darkening of the interior look by reason of external accidents; but with a silent heart, a humble look, yet mature and peaceful, let the mind, conscious in all things that it is well with it, preserve patience. And so much the more broadly, let it extend itself and pour forth love, as by such contrary things a broader way is opened to it, so as to feel nothing, show nothing, save what is redolent of charity. Thus also in wholeness of heart let it enter into that interior most gentle feeling of Jesus, which He was wont to have and had in His Passion and conversation. With the greatest constancy therefore let a man abide in love, charity, truth, and all virtues; and whatever may happen, let these remain inviolable and unhurt, and so all things will contribute to profit and gain. Nay, even if all things shall be outwardly distorted, intricate, and disturbed, yet to the mind all things will be at rest, for it enjoyeth infinite latitude of inward love, and according to time, place, and cause, by meeting, yielding, or helping, it omitteth to show forth none of those things which belong to chaste love; so, namely, as to be a faithful instrument of love, ever prepared to go in and out, according as it requireth. Hence, reading, singing, prayer, meditation, consideration, operation, rest, and all other things it directeth to this one object, so that love may be inviolably preserved inwardly in the soul, and outwardly in the showing forth of good works. Hence also it extendeth itself to an infinite degree, and its oblations and vows, and all the good that it doeth, are done and shall be done by offering them in one simple look liberally to God.

Chapter XXXVIII.

That all men in general are to be embraced in truth and love.

"LET Him kiss me with the kiss of His mouth." Noble surely, and exceeding delicate is the Bridegroom Jesus, Who is not joined in fruition to the soul that is taken up or burdened with any other thing whatsoever, because He hath nothing at all in common with what is accidental. Therefore, in as noble and sublime a way as is possible, let it strive to enjoy and be united to its Bridegroom Jesus, in that love by which He enjoyeth Himself, above and beyond all thought and comprehensibility. Hence in wholeness of heart, reverently and with great faith, ought we to stand before our Lord, and greedily to thirst after and drink deep draughts of His living and warm

Blood, by which we embrace all men and draw them into Jesus, Who is the Word, so that we may be united in Him; and by which also we are moved to suffer for His Name every kind of inconvenience and wrong, and are moved not to consider what we suffer from other men, whether it be behaviour or bodily infirmity, for we shall not be mindful for ever of infirmities, impediments, feebleness and imperfections, in all of which alike we now groan, and with which we contend. And because we are wholly ignorant how acceptable and glorious each man is, or will be before our Lord, on account of the man's perfection and purity, we can do nothing better than frequently to set aside everything unfavourable, and embrace all men in truth and love, and enjoy them in God, as those with whom we shall live for ever, and to strive to unite them to the Heart of Jesus, in the highest degree, especially those amongst us, who now seem to be less perfect and devout. But meanwhile, as long as we live here in the midst of innumerable storms and tempests, let the voice of each heart, in its own tune, and in its own measure, and in its own place, ceaselessly resound in the highest before the Throne. And let the fragrance also of spotless conversation, and of most chaste desires, pour forth its sweet savour like everlasting incense, and redound to its own principle; so that as the heavens have dropped with honey by the admirable advent of the Word of God, the Bridegroom, Jesus, in the flesh, and by the daily presenting Himself upon the altar, and by the frequent pouring forth of His Holy Spirit and of spiritual beauty on the souls of the elect; even so in their measure let the desires of each ascend on every side, correspond everywhere with grace, and extend themselves and their love one towards another into infinite latitude.

Chapter XXXIX.

What it is that chiefly unburdeneth and rendereth the heart free.

NOTHING so unburdeneth the heart, and rendereth it free, and maketh it to converse so freely without any narrowness before our Lord; and nothing so causeth recollection in the interior man after divers external distractions, and multiplied cares, as in all things, interior and exterior, temporal or eternal, to be led by no selfish cupidity, or self-seeking, nor to be bent by any private desire or affection towards any side: but whatever shall appear to be for the greater glory of God and the common good, safety and peace, to follow after this with one's whole strength, whether it be convenient or troublesome. This solidity of soul doth not make a man want or shun one thing or another, great or small; nay, rather he is able (or he knoweth how*) to see all things, hear, consider, and weigh whatever is said or done against him, and what is good or evil in others, that is to say, what is done in injury, or derogation to, or in lessening, or to the inconvenience, contempt, and lowering of himself; or, on the other hand, what tendeth to his honour and exaltation, and yet to be affected in neither case. Hence he poureth not forth his interior upon sensual goods, but passeth through to the internal fruition of the simple truth, and of chastest love, so that one is not impeded by the other, but in each the soul is with our Lord all in all.

---

* "Possit." Strange reads "potius scit."

To God be Praise, Honour and Glory.

THE END.

Richardson and Son, Printers, Derby.

www.ingramcontent.com/pod-product-compliance
Lightning Source LLC
Chambersburg PA
CBHW020252170426
43202CB00008B/334